OPERATION EXCELLENCE

———— ★ ————

Succeeding in Business and Life—
The U.S. Military Way

Mark Bender
Lieutenant Colonel, U.S. Army, Retired

⊹AMACOM

American Management Association
New York • Atlanta • Brussels • Chicago • Mexico City
San Francisco • Shanghai • Tokyo • Toronto • Washington, D. C.

Special discounts on bulk quantities of AMACOM books are available to corporations, professional associations, and other organizations. For details, contact Special Sales Department, AMACOM, a division of American Management Association, 1601 Broadway, New York, NY 10019.
Tel.: 212-903-8316. Fax: 212-903-8083.
Web site: www.amacombooks.org

This publication is designed to provide accurate and authoritative information in regard to the subject matter covered. It is sold with the understanding that the publisher is not engaged in rendering legal, accounting, or other professional service. If legal advice or other expert assistance is required, the services of a competent professional person should be sought.

Library of Congress Cataloging-in-Publication Data
Bender, Mark C. (Mark Christian), 1951–
Operation excellence : success strategies of the US military that will give you the winning edge in business and in life / Mark Bender.—1st ed.
        p. cm.
        Includes bibliographical references and index.
    ISBN 0-8144-0822-2
    1. Success.   2. Military art and science—United States—Miscellanea.
I. Title.
    BJ1611.2.B445 2004
    158.1—dc22   2003025535

Printing number

10 9 8 7 6 5 4 3 2 1

To Marilyn Bender

Whose analysis of Ulysses S. Grant's eastern campaign was key to my fifth-grade Civil War project. She gave me my love of books, and an appreciation for the challenges and lessons of life.

Always looking to expand her own comfort zone, she trekked to Israel to assist the Israeli Army in her seventies. She could observe a spartan display of military barracks life at San Juan Capistrano and remark, "Maybe they wanted it that way."

This project was conceived beside the pool of her California complex.

Thanks, Mom.

CONTENTS

FOREWORD

I met Mark Bender at lunch before baseball's All-Star game in Chicago in 1990. NFL coaching great Tom Landry was the featured speaker for the players that day, and Mark had just arrived from Europe. His baggage hadn't caught up with him and he had borrowed a green jacket. Tanned and athletic looking, I assumed he'd just won the Master's Golf Tournament.

The atmosphere was electric with excitement as we walked into the Hyatt Hotel restaurant. We were just starting to enjoy our pregame lunch when Tom Landry asked to join us. What an opportunity to learn from one of the great visionary leaders of the twentieth century.

Mark was intense, not missing a word of Landry's championship thinking. I realized later he was gathering information for what would become part of his book, *Train Tough the Army Way*, linking military thinking, planning, and training to the world of sports.

But that would have to wait. Two weeks later the Iraqis invaded Kuwait, and Colonel Bender was given the responsibility of helping to assemble the Army's dream team that would go into Iraq to defeat the Republican Guard. What an unbelievable pace to keep! Within days, to go from lunch with Landry to the call of "Play ball" and then to prepare the troops to dance with Saddam.

Regardless of the circumstance, Mark has always kept his unique sense of humor and indomitable confidence—qualities that have also made him a great writer and motivational speaker. He comes by these traits honestly. His dad, Sam Bender, is the dean of professional sports motivational speakers and has mentored me throughout my career. Sam is what I call a "people person."

Like father, like son. Mark spent his military career in the people part of the business—assignments, career development, promotions—and the reward system. He understands bureaucracy and how to bend it through force of will. More important, he understands people and what spurs them to optimal performance. His three years in NATO gave him a unique perspective of the international environment, working with our British, Dutch, and German allies. It came as no surprise when he was selected Officer of the Year for Headquarters, Allied Forces Central Europe. Mark's team-building skills are effective, regardless of culture and accent.

Like millions of Americans, I stand in awe of the United States Military. For the longest time I've wondered, "How do they do that?"

I'm glad Colonel Mark Bender has provided the answers, removed the mysteries, and presented his strategies in terms a nonmilitary mind can understand and draw inspiration from. Upon reflection, it's not surprising that our great military is built on fundamentals, the same basic truths that drive success in business—or any organization.

It makes a lot of sense to take what our military has learned and apply it to business, health, and our personal lives. Soldiers, sailors, airmen, and marines are products of the most sophisticated learning institutions on earth. They work in a life-or-death environment. Their success, and the esteem in which they are held, is unparalleled. Clearly, they have something to share, and clearly, Mark Bender is just the guy to make the translation for us.

As a speaker and writer, it's fair to say I work in the communications industry. This year I'll log over 150,000 miles for about 200 speaking opportunities. That's 200 days on the road. Between books and tapes, I have about 20 media products on the market. So communication is dear to my heart. For me, it's a career.

But communication is central to everything we do. It's central to relationships and to every aspect of a business endeavor. A lot of problems are resolved through communication—it's the only way great ideas ever go anywhere. I think you'll find Colonel Bender's approach in this arena to be refreshing—speak less, say more.

Another thing I see as I steer around the country is the struggle to establish values. It's true with churches, college and professional sports teams, and Fortune 500 companies. No matter how high you climb, you'll find a series of ethical dilemmas facing you. It's something you never outgrow, but that you can prepare for by committing to consistently making right choices—otherwise known as forming good habits. Without principles, life quickly degenerates into an endless series of shortcuts, and we fall short of our best possibilities.

You'll find the military approach to values enlightening. It's good to know our guys train just as hard in this area as they do in any other. Values training and ethical decision making is just as tough as taking a hill. It calls for discipline and dedication.

I'm thrilled that you're involved with Mark Bender's strategies.

It means that you're proactive. You're about to make something happen.

I'm not much of a military strategist, so I'll just agree with Mark on one important point: "Move. Move. Move."

And communicate.

Good luck as you prepare to move out!

Van Crouch
Van Crouch Communications

INTRODUCTION

The greatest pleasure is to vanquish your enemies and chase them before you, to rob them of their wealth and to see those dear to them bathed in tears, to ride their horses and clasp to your bosom their wives and daughters.
                                                    —Genghis Khan

My friend, we live in a dangerous world. The spirit of Genghis Khan lives on in a thousand permutations across planet Earth. Would that it were not so.

Most of us grew up under the shadow of nuclear missiles. It's not something we think about every day. But the fact that we don't think about it doesn't change the reality of their existence. In the space of a half hour we could all be toast. The specter of weapons of mass destruction in the hands of terrorists is something new to think about.

Life is tough. Reality can be too ugly to deal with on a moment-to-moment, day-to-day basis. It isn't fair. There are no guarantees. Everything we do carries existential risk.

Have you contemplated your own mortality lately? Because when you stare death in the face for a few minutes it has a wonderfully enlightening quality. You begin to appreciate life and the finite amount of time you have to live it. We have X amount of time, and, just like in algebra class, X is unknown. This isn't morbid or even depressing, it's just a fact of life. I don't know about you, but I'm going down swinging.

Use this book as an instrument to discover truth. Before you can change your life you've got to get to the truth. You *can* handle the truth. And the truth *will* set you free. This book is like a mirror—to view where you are today and to formulate how you're going to get where you want to be tomorrow.

Subject what's here to rigorous examination. But suspend some of the preconceptions that inevitably come up about the military. If you'll do that you'll find *Operation Excellence* can be a vehicle to change your life.

But you've got to get beyond Sergeant Bilko, Gomer Pyle, and the guys on *M*A*S*H*. OK, that stuff is funny. All right, hilarious. Some of it's even true. But it masks the larger truth of the important processes that take place in our military. That's why so many of our success strategies are, in effect, *secret*. Nobody's made the translation from what we do to excel in a life-or-death industry to what works in business and life. Until now.

I'll be your translator, guru, and guide—think of me with love beads if you want to. Of course, sometimes I'll put on my drill sergeant hat to make sure you're staying motivated. My concern is not just what you think, but how you think. Because if we can impact how you think, we can impact your actions, and ultimately, the quality of your life.

I'm offering a way in. Not the only way in, certainly, but a way in nonetheless.

I'm out to influence your attitude.

I want to blast open a new way of thinking and light your fire. I want to give you strategies that will, in fact, change your life. I'm going to be chucking hand grenades and laying down machine gun fire to get you moving. And you don't have to join the military to reap the benefit. I've already done that for you.

★ ★ ★   STRATEGY 1   ★ ★ ★

COMMIT TO THE TRUTH. Subject all things to rigorous examination. The U.S. Military is a success story because, even despite the politics and rivalries, we have learned to seek and accept the truth about ourselves, our capabilities, and our enemies. The truth demands a response. That's when the real work begins.

The United States Military

You Built It, You Paid for It, Now You're Getting Something Back!

Have you ever wondered why the United States has the greatest military force on earth, but has a struggling public education system?

How is it that the same democracy gets one kind of results in one area and a completely different set of results in another?

Most strangely, how is it that the U.S. Military is able to take the product of our education system and produce a winner? It's mind-boggling.

The answer is that we educate—aggressively. From the moment a person enters military service to the day he retires, he's in a highly structured learning environment. He starts out in training, and there's more training at every level to which he advances. Soldiers, sailors, airmen, and marines are trained every day in their units and given every possible incentive for self-education. It's relentless. There's a tremendous emphasis in the U.S. Military on the value of education. We spend half our lives in school, and the other half is spent training. We have to learn how to learn.

We're in a life-or-death business. We're focused.

The U.S. profession of arms is focused on measurable results. It's critical that our people know how to think, how to lead, and how to work as a team. We're open to better ideas, whether these ideas come from our understanding of the past or the cutting edge of futuristic thinking. Our people learn the principles of war, but they also learn how to innovate, when to throw out the book and create. Our work is done under pressure—we're challenged mentally, physically, and spiritually. The finest learning institutions in the world belong to the United States Military. Period. Bar none.

The United States Military is very, very good at changing people's lives. We do behavioral modification as a matter of course. We're in the transformation business, the business of taking raw recruits and molding them into soldiers, sailors, airmen, or marines. That's what we do.

One day I asked a couple of questions: "What if we could bottle what it is we do that takes goofed-up kids and turns them into marines? How can we endow people with marine-like qualities without them ever leaving home?"

The answers were not that profound. The answers turned out to be simple. We could reach people through their thinking! We could take the principles of military training, jazz them around a bit, and present a program with dynamic breakthrough power—the power to transform lives. The result is *Operation Excellence*, based on tried and tested success strategies of the U.S. Military that have stood the test of time.

Apply the strategies to strengthen your personal drive, willpower, and initiative. This is your chance to think like a marine without all the commotion. It's not effort-free and it doesn't cure arthritis, but it's a great way to get yourself focused and on the road to a better life.

Military thinking is a way into something deeper. It's a path to that state of excellence we all seek. It's not for everybody and it's not the only way. The 50 strategies is a program of instruction designed to get you fired up and moving forward. Like a drill sergeant, I'm going to be yelling "Move, Move, Move!" at every opportunity. If I'm doing my job properly, you're going to love me and hate me at the same time. It's going to be us against mediocrity. You and me against a world of comfort and complacency. It would be easier to sit back and let the world pass us by. But we're not going to do that.

We're going to get up in the face of life and demand a response. We're going to work hard, work smart, and take the hill. Yes, there's a certain amount of effort involved. That's where Discipline comes in. That's right, Discipline with a capital *D*. Discipline is one of the bedrock support structures of the military success secrets. Motivation. Discipline. Confidence. Sacrifice. You get a chapter on each of the big four.

Like the washouts at boot camp, not everyone will make it. We're going to have some recycles, those who aren't ready right now, who need to come back at a later time when they're ready to take on the challenges. That's OK. The fact that you're reading this at all puts you way ahead of the power curve. If you're reading this it means you care enough to want to improve and that you're open to a new way to look at the world. That's an important first step.

★ ★ ★   **STRATEGY 2**   ★ ★ ★

PREPARE TO CHANGE. What if just one area of your life improved as a result of the 50 strategies? Would it be worth it? What if you got fired up and got a new edge to life? If you're not prepared to change, to improve, you're wasting your time. Change involves accepting discomfort, so be prepared for some pain as you move to the next level.

You see, military thinking is powerful, so powerful that people are afraid to use it. We don't want to become "militant"—and I agree with that. Instead, we want to leverage the positive qualities that come with military thought and leave the other stuff behind. A military mind-set can be used for good or bad. George Washington, Dwight Eisenhower, Colin Powell all used it to better the world. Adolf Hitler, Joseph Stalin, and Mao Tse-Tung went the other way. It's all in how you use it. The same strategies that guide the United States Military, strategies gleaned from the study of the art and science of warfare, are available to you—*strategies for changing your business, your body, and your life!*

It's About Personal Action

This isn't a book about political action; it's a book about personal action. It's not about skinheads, militia groups, or gun control. This isn't about combat, warfare, or killing. Nor is it an excuse to hate. Because what we do in the United States Military can be so devastating, we're very conscious of the moral consequences of every act. Later, we'll address ethical issues in detail, and, amazingly, it will not be boring. There's no excuse for boring.

This will not be a by-the-numbers training manual. The training manuals are already out there—and nobody's reading them except the people who have to. I'm going to give you my unique spin on the military mystique and encapsulate my philosophy in 50 strategies. You're going to get the secrets of military transformational power from someone who's been there. It's my job to translate for you, to take the "militarese" and break it down to where you can use it.

You're going to get a lot of my spin; I'm going to be the face that guides you through the process. I'll give you the stuff that works and skip the rest. Yes, the U.S. Military sometimes lives up to our reputation for the inane, but by the same token we do a lot of great things that even we don't fully understand. As I said, I'll be your guide.

Have you ever wondered why people join the U.S. Military in the first place? Why they leave home, risk danger, and give up personal freedom? I'll let you in on a big secret—because it's *fun*. F-U-N. Soldiers know how to have fun. And the minute we stop making it fun is when we start losing soldiers. We like shooting stuff up, blowing stuff up, and partying afterward. I'm not talking about war. War is hell, training is a blast. We do it safely and responsibly, but boy do we do it.

And that's the way this book is going to be. F-U-N. No sacred cows. If it needs to be said, we're going to say it. If it hacks somebody off, so be it. If it stops being fun, turn the page.

Studies show that the most effective way for a person to learn is from another living, breathing human being. That's why there will always be teachers. And as long as there are teachers there will be people trying to figure out what they are really trying to say. Ever been halfway through a class and you just have to stop and ask, "What are we trying to do here?" I don't want that to happen to you, so I'm going to tell you a few things about myself. I'm a different breed of cat.

I attended a pacifist nursery school, so naturally I wanted to play war games right from Jump Street. I wanted to compete, so I played sports my entire life. When I drew a low number in the draft lottery, I was forced to consider how I would fulfill my military obligation. I opted for officer training and was commissioned as a second lieutenant in the United States Army in 1974. I was less than excited about being in the Army, but it grew on me. Grew on me to the point where I am now convinced that the secrets—the strategies—of military thought processes need to be made available to everyone. I see it as my job to do just that.

Midway through my career I was privileged to attend the Command and General Staff College at Fort Leavenworth, Kansas. It's one of the best learning environments on earth. Pershing, Patton, and MacArthur attended there, to name a few. So did Schwartzkopf and Colin Powell. But the experience of Dwight D. Eisenhower at the college intrigued me the most—so much so that I wrote a book on the subject. Eisenhower was told by the higher-ups that he wasn't ready for the school and would "probably fail," yet he rose to be the number one graduate in his class—an achievement that shot his career out of neutral and onto a track that propelled him to the presidency. I love that kind of stuff.

Later in my career I returned to Fort Leavenworth, where I mentored young officers at the U.S. Army's premier problem-solving school. And there's no better way to learn than to teach.

When I left active duty a few years ago, the first thing I did was team up with Tex Winter, the inventor of basketball's triangle offense. Tex had been in coaching for more than fifty years, had coached Michael Jordan longer than any other coach, and had six NBA championship rings with the Chicago Bulls. He's since gone on to win three more with Phil Jackson in Los Angeles. The book was called *Trial By Basketball*, a fitting title I thought, because the more I looked behind the championships, the more the struggles became apparent. It whetted my appetite for delving more deeply into the world of sports performance and resulted in a strange synthesis—merging the world of the athlete with that of the soldier.

I felt uniquely equipped to write *Train Tough the Army Way: 50 Sports Strategies to Out-Think, Out-Train, and Out-Perform Your Competition*. It was the work I'd been preparing my whole life to undertake. I'd spent half a lifetime on the field, in the gym, and at the track competing and doing the hard work that victory demands. Baseball, basketball, and volleyball were my mainstays—but I also played or coached football, soccer, wrestling, European handball, sprints and distance running, weight lifting, golf, and tennis. I once figured I'd spent 75 seasons playing team sports— and that was before I was 50.

Train Tough the Army Way was a powerful mix of sports tactics and military strategies, historical vignettes, and transformational power. I strongly recommend it for anyone who competes on the friendly fields of strife. It takes military planning, training techniques, and leadership and team-building skills and applies them to sports, laying the groundwork for what now follows.

As I said in *Train Tough,* I'm a guy who believes the history of the universe is reducible to the back of a 3- by 5-inch card. I like to keep things simple. To my mind, if most of the learning situations in life lasted half as long, they would be twice as effective. *Operation Excellence* is short and sweet for exactly that reason.

At the end of each chapter is a Train Tough Challenge. Take these challenges. I won't ask you to do anything I wouldn't do or haven't already done. Get used to meeting challenges. You're going to face a lot of them before you're through. Meet the Train Tough Challenges as we move along and, by the end, you'll be ready to take on the world.

But enough intro. It's time to move out. We're going to attack the bad guys of comfort, lethargy, and "good enough." It's gut-check time. Grab your gear and prepare for a fire mission. We're going all the way live in OPERATION MOTIVATION. See you there.

★ ★ ★   **STRATEGY 3**   ★ ★ ★

ACCEPT CHALLENGE. Get used to meeting challenges, that's how muscle is built, both mental and physical. Military training is conducted under pressure. It's a life-or-death business. We're challenged mentally, physically, and spiritually. Meet the Train Tough Challenges as we move along. By the end, you'll be ready to take on the world.

Train Tough Challenge

Read on.

PART ONE

—— ★ ——

THE ARSENAL OF VICTORY

Motivation. Discipline. Confidence. Sacrifice.
Sharpen the weapons in your arsenal.

1

---★---

OPERATION MOTIVATION

You Can't Say No to the Drill Sergeant

It is not enough to fight. It is the spirit which we bring to the fight that decides the issue. It is morale that wins the victory.
—General George Marshall

I hadn't been at Army Boot Camp more than a few hours when I started asking myself, "How do I get out of this?"

There really wasn't an honorable way out. I was stuck. There was nowhere to go but forward.

The drill sergeant got into me right off the bat, correctly identifying me as someone who needed extra work. Nothing in my experience had adequately prepared me for the sheer discomfort of his presence for the next six weeks. He spit out rewards and punishments like machine gun fire. He pressed his barrel chest right up against me and put his huge head right in my face as he explained things. Worse, he had standards. And there was no way around him.

He was *loud*. He was *excitable*. The smallest things were of earth-shattering importance. His energy was unflagging. He ran us everywhere. We did push-ups for punishment and push-ups as a reward.

He told us to follow only lawful orders, that nothing the Army told us to do relieved us of the obligation to think. I kept waiting for an unlawful order from my drill sergeant. It never came.

My drill sergeant was supremely confident. My drill sergeant was technically competent. There was no task he gave us that he couldn't have performed better himself. I could not say no to the drill sergeant. Despite our strained "relationship," he earned my trust.

He made it clear the gate to graduation went through him. We were either going to be the best platoon in Charlie Company or we weren't going anywhere. And the only way we were going to be the best platoon in Charlie Company was to work as a team. Our motto became "Cooperate and Graduate."

As our team developed, he raised the standards. But a funny thing happened. As we became self-motivated, his approach changed, and we began working as much for our buddies as we did for him. By graduation we were ready to take on the world—together.

That drill sergeant was the best thing that ever happened to me. My drill sergeant demonstrated the kind of energy, drive, and bedrock motivation it would take to navigate the competitive shoals of the United States Military. In the end, he was an inspiration. At the time, I thought he was just a pain in the end.

I have to laugh when I hear executives tell their staffs, "No drill sergeants!" These guys obviously never had drill sergeants. If they had, they'd be hiring drill sergeants.

★ ★ ★   **STRATEGY 4**   ★ ★ ★

HARNESS THE POWER OF SHOCK. History is replete with cultures and human beings responding to shock. Think of the United States after Pearl Harbor. Shock got us focused. Shock got us moving. But the greater challenge is to conceptualize shocking scenarios and prepare accordingly. Get ahead of the shock curve and anticipate—then feed off the energy. Attune to life's minishocks. Use them for motivation.

Human Motivation 101

Let's begin with a brief discussion of human motivation.

Was it not Abraham Maslow who developed Maslow's hierarchy of needs? The name so indicates, although it may have been Abe's brother, Moe.

In any event, the hierarchy helps explain what makes people do the things we do.

First, we must eat. Most of us eat too much, so we can pretty much take this one for granted.

Second, we want to feel safe—even if we aren't. We want to feel that life is predictable and orderly, and that bad things won't get us.

Third, we want to belong, to find love and gain a sense of self-esteem, perhaps through achievement.

Last, if there's any energy left, we want to self-actualize, to have the sense that we're living up to our potential.

All of human motivation can pretty well be jammed into one of these four categories—unless you refer to the motivation chapter of your typical Psychology 101 textbook. If you do, you'll find twelve pages on sexual motivation, ten pages on hunger and eating disorders, six pages on achievement motivation, and a couple pages on the need to belong (where, you may be interested to note, a one-paragraph discussion of religious motivation takes place). You will definitely not find God in the index.

When you boil it all down you find that action is always preceded by motivation. When you're after peak performance you've got to be hungry. The lion hunts only when it's hungry.

Human sexuality is also a powerful force. But our libido is not just the seat of our sexual passion, it also drives our passion for life. Passion and desire are at the heart of our ambitions. We're built with the drive to achieve and to find our place at the conference table, to be part of a team.

It's actually pretty simple. The question is, how can we harness these basic motivations and propel ourselves forward at a higher speed?

The answer is that motivation needs props—structures to hold us up when the going gets tough, when internal or external stress threatens to overwhelm our motivation.

One of these props is *shock*. The doctor tells you to quit smoking or you'll be dead in a year. A bully kicks sand in your face at the beach. Terrorists launch an attack. Shocking events wake us up to reality. Used correctly, shock gets us moving. But the greater challenge is to get ahead of the shock curve, to be strong enough and smart enough to deter bullies and terrorists and to avoid bad news from the doctor.

That leads us to *belief.* What do you believe in? Mom? Apple pie? The American way? Do you believe in God?

Your beliefs impact your motivation.

Take the guy who really doesn't believe in anything. No God. Love stinks. Whatever will be will be. How motivated would you expect that guy to be?

I'm not going to tell you what to believe. I am going to tell you that you better find out what those beliefs are and harness them.

Until you have harnessed your beliefs, you aren't ready to go on the *quest,* the ultimate motivational prop. Without beliefs, life is spectator sport. Beliefs put you in the saddle, ready to move out. If nothing else, believe you can make a difference. Believe that your honest effort can make the world a better place. Join the team.

Look, I know there's a lot of philosophy out there telling you to just sit around and watch the world go by. Eliminate your desires and lower your expectations. That stuff has its place, but it's not my schtick. To me, that's called a *vacation.* Any idiot can go on vacation. I'm here to get you moving. Would you need me to tell you how to sit on your butt? I don't think so.

A quest mentality gets you moving. Seeing your life as a quest provides a focus and direction the rest of the crowd doesn't have. You establish goals, your core beliefs jack up your motivation, and you're ready for some earth-shattering challenges.

You supply the goals. Whatever works for you.

When they asked George Mallory why he wanted to climb Mount Everest, he answered simply, "Because it's there."

It helps to know what's there before you establish your goals.

Mallory saw the mountain. Mother Teresa saw poverty. Jerry Lewis saw sick kids that needed help. Maybe you see 40 pounds of fat. Whatever.

The point is to see what's there for you and turn it into a quest. Consecrate yourself to the mission. Have high expectations for what you can accomplish. See yourself in a fight to the finish. Get ready to push yourself beyond your old limits.

★ ★ ★ **STRATEGY 5** ★ ★ ★

HARNESS THE POWER OF *BELIEF.* Until you have harnessed your beliefs, you aren't ready to go on the quest. Without belief, life is a spectator sport. What do you believe? On what basis do you hold these beliefs? What you believe impacts your motivation. Your core beliefs are those truths you have validated over and over again. Know what they are.

Sink or Swim?

At 12:14 A.M. on July 30, 1945, with 1,199 men aboard, the USS *Indianapolis* was torpedoed by a Japanese submarine. Twelve minutes later she sank. Some 900 men survived the initial explosions and fire and were cast into the shark-infested waters of the Philippine Sea. Only after five terrible days were all the survivors picked up. Without food or water, exposed to the elements and the attacking sharks, only 317 men lived to tell the tale. If you saw the movie *Jaws,* you'll recall the old fisherman's gut-wrenching recollection of the nightmare.

Responses to the crisis varied widely from one sailor to another. The men hit the water in varying states of mental and physical distress. Some were injured or burned; some had life jackets and others did not. Some gathered in teams and fought to keep each other alive. Leadership and sacrifice played key roles in saving the lives of many. Every man aboard the USS *Indianapolis,* whether he survived or perished, paid a tremendous price to defend our freedom—reminding us of the endless horrors of war.

Imagine yourself floating alone in the ocean, abandoned. No need to worry about sharks or how you came to be there. But you're alone, with land many miles off.

What assets do you have?

Let's take inventory.

You have your mind, your brain. Your mind has stored information on survival situations, shipwreck stories, and your ability to swim. Your brain functions as a product of your experiences—and training. Inside your mind are your decision-making and problem-solving faculties, the machinery to help you decide whether to swim for land or to float as long as possible in the hope of being picked up. Your mind is synonymous with your heart, reflecting the level of toughness, determination, and emotional control you bring to the situation.

The state of your body might be critical. Is it fit? Have you eaten recently? Are you hydrated?

What is your level of hope?

Do you have friends or family who will surely be searching for you?

Are you feeling lucky?

Do you believe in God?

How long you survive will likely be determined by the answers to these questions. Reduced to floating protoplasm, we have an excellent opportunity to take a look at ourselves.

What do you have to live for? Have you pretty much seen and done it all? Do you feel that your mission in life is complete? Maybe your time has come. Letting go won't be so hard. Maybe it's time to go.

Or maybe you still have work to do, and people who depend on you. You're a fighter by nature, and this is just one more crazy situation to work your way out of. Something to overcome.

★ ★ ★ STRATEGY 6 ★ ★ ★

INVENTORY YOUR ASSETS. What is the state of your mind? Your body? Your relationships? Your career? In the military we make inventory a continuous process. We always want to know where our people and equipment are, and whether they're ready for battle. Take stock of your assets, so you can fully access them on your quest.

One Tough Sissy

Captain Harry Truman had no business serving in World War I. He was practically blind in one eye, wearing thick, corrective glasses from age 8. Harry memorized the eye chart so he could join the Army, a patriotic act of self-sacrifice almost beyond our imagination today.

Throughout the war Truman carried in his breast pocket a picture of Bess Wallace, the only woman he would ever love. He first saw Bess at age 6 in Sunday School, and it was love at first sight. Bashful around girls, it would take Harry five years to get up the courage to actually speak to young Bess, who came from a well-to-do family. Harry came from a family that struggled to make ends meet; they lacked the social standing of the Wallaces. Bess was athletic, described as "a hell of a third baseman and tennis player." Harry couldn't play games because of his eyes; he played the piano and was looked upon as a sissy.

Harry was 26 when he began courting Bess in earnest. He visited her on Sundays and kept up a steady letter-writing campaign from the family farm south of town. But Bess had the pick of a wide field, and her mother was sure she could do better than Harry.

He proposed marriage in one of his letters. She politely declined. He wrote back and thanked her for not ridiculing him—and continued the barrage. He fashioned a grass tennis court and threw a party for her. She didn't come. But the letters and visits continued. After two more years Bess finally admitted that if she ever were to marry, she would marry Harry. It was a big if, but there was hope.

If only he could find his fortune. . . .

Harry borrowed money to mine for zinc in Oklahoma. The enterprise failed. He borrowed more money to drill for oil. The well went bust and Harry sold his stake. The company continued, dug a little deeper, and struck it rich. At age 33, Harry Truman was penniless and a failure.

As Harry prepared to serve his country in World War I, Bess Wallace finally agreed to his marriage proposal. This time it was Harry who said no, he didn't want to subject Bess to marriage with a "prospective cripple."

But Harry Truman returned whole and with renewed confidence from his military success. Among other feats, he commanded Battery B of the Second Battalion, 129th Field Artillery—a unit that fired 10,000 rounds in numerous engagements—without losing a soldier. Harry was now a leader of men, described by one of his soldiers as "one tough son of a bitch of a man."

Six weeks after returning home from France, Harry and Bess were wed. The marriage would last their lifetimes, persevering through numerous trials and tribulations.

Harry Truman was persistent. Harry Truman was determined. Harry Truman had character. And those same qualities that ruled his love life would take him to the White House—as president and commander in chief. When Harry Truman locked on a target he was one tough sissy.

How Bad Do You Want It?

In *Train Tough the Army Way,* a book about cutting-edge sports strategies, I introduced one of life's key questions—"How bad do you want it?"

At the time, I saw this question mainly in terms of sports motivation. It's a simple technique in which players ask themselves that question before stepping up to the plate in baseball, approaching the free throw line in basketball, or breaking out of the huddle before a field goal attempt in football. The object is to give a one-word answer—"BAD."

Crystallizing motivation in a single word, one that you believe in, is like pulling the lanyard on an artillery gun. *Boom!* You're ready for action. In *action,* motivation overcomes the twin monsters of fear and self-consciousness. Effective action is guided by reasoning and imagination. But, in a word, you've got to want it—BAD.

Looking at the courtship of Harry and Bess Truman, I realized that the how-bad-do-you-want-it question applies to all of life. Too often we lollygag through our daily routines, never having identified the things that are important to us. We're not focused. We haven't put a value on things. We don't know how bad we want it, until it's too late.

Harry Truman put a value on his woman and the type of relationship he would share with her. He worked a good part of his lifetime to win her hand. The man was motivated.

Harry Truman also had values. He could have settled for second best. He could have avoided World War I, or even married Bess before he went overseas. But he made the tough choices. The man definitely had values.

What do you value?

And how bad do you want it?

★ ★ ★ **STRATEGY 7** ★ ★ ★

DEVELOP A QUEST MENTALITY. You're not just sitting there, waiting for the world to come to you. You're on a quest. Know what that quest is. Ultimately, battles are won by going over to the offense, with all the risk of failure that comes with taking action. The quest mentality is one of the most powerful forces known to man. It will guide you through and around obstacles and into the unstoppable zone.

Welcome to First Platoon, Charlie Company

There's nothing like a drill sergeant's welcome to boot camp. Mine was highly motivational. There was no doubt in my military mind what my drill sergeant expected. Here's what he said.

I want the First Platoon to be the best platoon in Charlie Company. You're here to push beyond your limits. Don't even think about half-stepping; you're in a fight to the finish.

No obsessing!

No whining!

Look to your motivation, people, fire up. Dive in all the way. Know what you believe and start acting on those beliefs. Consecrate yourself. Raise expectations.

We thrive on adversity here. Knock us down, we get back up. Again and again and again and again. We never give up. We're just plain tougher than the guys in Second Platoon.

We're hungry. We know that life is just one shock after another. But it's shock that keeps us going. That ain't ever gonna stop. "Thanks, I needed that," we say, one shock after another.

Shock is just a thing when you believe. Shock is just a thing when you're on a quest.

We're moving out. We're loading up. We're on a quest.

We gonna be the best platoon in Charlie Company. Everything we do, we overdo. It's true—we do more before nine o'clock in the morning than the other people do all day.

We're crazy. But we're disciplined crazy.

We know that all the motivation in the world is nothing without the discipline to hold it up. Discipline. Extraordinary moment-by-moment discipline.

Now get *MOVING!*

Train Tough Challenge

Define your *quest*. What were you put here on planet Earth to master?

_____

_____

_____

How bad do you want it?

_____

_____

_____

Jot down the next three steps of your QUEST.

1. _____

2. _____

3. _____

Take the first step!

2

★

DISCIPLINE

It's Habit Forming

Above all discipline; eternally, and inevitably, discipline. Discipline is
the screw, the nail, the cement, the glue, the nut, the bolt, the rivet that
holds everything tight.

—Private Gerald Gersh

We're fat. Out of shape. Addicted. Divorced. And in debt. Rather than work things out, we sue each other. We're watching TV, playing video games, and having sex on the Internet. But we're pressed for time.

People don't always like to hear what I have to say. They want to hear, "You're fine. It's not your fault."

Well it's not fine. We have serious problems. And until we perceive the forces that are holding us back, we're going to continue down the highway to mediocrity. We like to say America's the greatest nation on earth. But great for what? Canada's bigger. China's got more people. And I can tell you from personal experience that the quality of just about everything is better in Europe.

OK, we have the greatest military on the face of the earth, which is why I'm writing this book from the military perspective in the first place. But is that enough? Shouldn't we be leading in some other areas as well?

This summer we had a sixteen-year-old houseguest from Switzerland. It was embarrassing. The U.S. carrier got him here three hours late and lost his luggage. The highway I drove him home on looked like something in a Third World country. When we arrived back home there was no water pressure.

For three weeks I saw America through the eyes of a sixteen-year-old from Switzerland, and it was not a pretty sight. There's a lot of broken, beat-up stuff here, and I had a lot of explaining to do. And of course I did it all in English, not French, German, or Italian, which the kid could've understood just as well.

He did like our ketchup, hamburgers, movies, music, and video games. We lead the world in fatty foods and goofing around.

But you know what? We choose how we live. We're sitting on third base in this country when we ought to be streaking toward home.

It's not enough to talk about democracy and our system of government. How well are we executing? In elections we have trouble just counting the votes. We're sleepwalking. We've built a culture that rewards nonachievement, where mediocrity is an end in itself.

The good news is that for those few who catch fire, the sky's the limit. That's why people still flock here. Opportunity. The immigrants see what we don't. They see opportunities that the rest of us are ignoring.

Hey, the only person you control is you. You can influence others, but it still comes back to you. This is not a book about social or political action. It's a book about personal action.

At the end of his stay, the Swiss kid asked me whether I'd rather live in the United States or Europe. "Of course I want to live in the United States," I told him. "You think I'm crazy!"

I keep my doubts at the water's edge. We're still the land of opportunity.

Self-Discipline—Yeah, You!

If you think back to high school, you probably remember the roughneck who didn't fit in. When problems developed with his parents and teachers, he up and joined the Marines, and got the heck out of town.

The next time you saw the guy he was a different person. Ramrod straight, short haircut, low body fat, new muscle. Sense of purpose.

It's mind-blowing. Here's the guy who had trouble controlling himself, the guy people saw as a problem child going nowhere, and now he's back on leave with a new look—and a new attitude.

From experience, I can tell you that a lot of kids like that are made for the military. They know deep down in their hearts that they need a wake-up call, and a cause to get them on track. For whatever reason they've gone down the wrong road and need shock treatment to get turned around.

We give it to them. We change lives. That's our business.

Not everybody makes it, but for those who genuinely want to get out of a rut, there's nothing like the challenge of a life-or-death business to get you focused, energized, and moving forward.

What we give kids is enforced discipline. Maybe they were getting away with murder at home and in high school. Not here. We're going to attend to details in a way they've never seen before. They're going to be highly motivated to get it right, because the penalties for getting it wrong are swift and uncompromising.

We've even got our own disciplinary system, the Uniform Code of Military Justice. It's fair, but streamlined. When recruits raise their right hand to take the oath, we've got them. Welcome aboard. Keep your nose clean.

We're going to teach them how to stand, how to walk, and how to talk. We wake them up with a whistle or by banging a trash can lid. No, you can't sleep in. You don't just make your bed; here, you make it our way. You store your stuff, your personal effects, the way we tell you to. You do push-ups our way, and you do a lot of them.

We realized a long time ago that discipline is the platform from which we launch success. If the platform is solid, the sky's the limit. We know that every discipline affects every other discipline. They build on each other. The devil is in the details, so we pay a lot of attention to details. We know that human beings have to force themselves to be disciplined; we like to think we're here to help.

There are huge benefits for those who are disciplined. Discipline builds an environment of continuous improvement. We learn the secrets of delayed gratification through discipline, and we gain appreciation for the benefits of freedom by willingly giving them up for a while. There are no happier marines than those who have earned their first weekend pass. Ultimately, we learn that discipline allows and facilitates freedom.

Hardship and adversity are the training grounds of discipline. We're a little old-fashioned in that regard. The ancient Greeks saw discipline as one's training to take one's place in the world. The word *disciple,* with the same root, was one who left home, family, and possessions. The latin *disciplina* means instruction or knowledge. We go back.

And we always go back to meeting and exceeding baseline standards. Concentration. Effort. Determination. The mission above the comfort of self. The team pulling together for the good of the whole. "Me," and my desires, are not first anymore. It hurts, but it's wonderfully cleansing.

Discipline is the foundation on which we build. Sure, we live in a sophisticated, complex world. That's just the point—we need to establish discipline as the rock-solid foundation from which to ascend through levels of increasing complexity. Discipline at the start; discipline throughout.

★ ★ ★   **STRATEGY 8**   ★ ★ ★

GET CONTROL OF YOUR ENVIRONMENT. As you develop discipline, you gain control of your mind and your environment. Uncluttering your mind gives you greater access to your mental source of power. Get out ahead of life and arrange things to support the goals you want to accomplish. The environment of continuous improvement is sustained by discipline.

Reality Bites

Germany is a nice enough country, but during the tail end of the Cold War the duty was tough. We often had three times the mission and one-third the staff of a stateside operation. Change was rampant. Careers were made or broken there.

I took command of a personnel service company right before Desert Storm. The first thing we did was flunk an inspection. It was a good wake-up call, but for me it was strike one, adding to the pressure of a new command supporting 14,000 soldiers in ten locations. I could see this was a job that was going to take some overtime.

Desert Storm multiplied everything. Here we'd been planning to fight Russians from the east and now we were transporting thousands of soldiers to the Persian Gulf. We made it up as we went along.

Half my unit went to the Gulf, and as commander I picked up responsibility for two additional units where the commanders and most of the staff had gone forward. If you're doing the math here, we were doing an awful lot with very little.

As winter set in we grew more concerned about protecting our force from terrorist attack. In addition to their normal duties, my soldiers were spending more and more of their time on guard duty, patrolling streets in the bitter German cold. All our administrative systems were breaking down, as we devoted less and less time to their upkeep. None of the trans-actions that run the Army were taking place. How were our guys in the Gulf getting paid and promoted? Did we even know where our guys were? It was a nightmare.

On top of that we had the welfare of all the families left in Germany to consider. With so many soldiers forward in the Gulf, we had to do what we could to support the families left behind in a foreign country. It would also be our job to tell families if Dad or Mom became a casualty and to render appropriate support. It was almost unthinkable, but we had to train for it.

On the day the air war commenced, I got a call from one of my warrant officers informing me that we could not account for a pack of ID cards. There are one hundred cards in a pack. Losing a single ID card is a big deal. After all, the ID card is the key piece of identification used to gain access to a base and to identify friend or foe.

The warrant officer and I knew that the overwhelming likelihood was that we had a simple accounting problem on our hands. A lot of times the clerks made mistakes when they count the packs at the issue point. Still, there was the possibility the cards had been lost or stolen and could be used by the bad guys. Knowing full well it could cost me my career, I reported the problem to the military police—as well as to higher head-quarters.

That put us under investigation. Every move, past and present, was under review. It was excruciating. The pressure was unbelievable. For more than a year I started my day at 4:00 A.M. without having to wait for my alarm clock. I wasn't sleeping much then anyway. It was one foot in front of the other, day after day after day.

We were going so fast the screwups occurred by the minute. It was like triage in an emergency ward. I almost cracked.

It got worse when the war ended. As our troops returned from the Gulf, the personnel actions began in earnest. Our soldiers wouldn't be with us long. Operation Homeward Bound virtually emptied Germany of U.S. forces, another mission we accomplished on the fly. It was a brilliant stroke—sending units back to the United States with little more than a touchdown in Germany. Why not move them before they got comfort-able? It was a good idea but difficult to execute, and I once again found myself on the cutting edge of painful innovation.

We got the troops back to the States before the Germans knew what hit them. The malcontents preparing to protest continued U.S. presence in Europe never had a chance to make protest signs. All they heard was a giant sucking sound.

If war is hell, cleaning up in the aftermath is a close second. It taxed every resource I could summon—belief in God, support of family, faith in my fellow soldiers, and the rightness of our cause.

I don't invoke the benefits of discipline lightly, but discipline is the glue that holds the center together. I know from experience that reality bites, that we don't always have the luxury of a tidy battlefield. Discipline turns to perseverance in the flame of adversity. Situations sometimes reduce us to one foot in front of the other.

But perseverance is more than just survival. Perseverance is hitting back.

Even in the depths of my despair, with failure looming like a vulture, I knew discipline demanded counterattack. My military training taught me to move forward at all costs, even to "fail forward faster" if that's what it took.

It was my job to inspire, to exude confidence, and to set the example. When I could no longer do that, the Army would replace me with someone who could. I wasn't about to let that happen.

I learned a lot from that difficult time in my life. Among other things, I learned that all the difficulties faced in those two years were not worth the challenge of a single morning at Valley Forge.

★ ★ ★ STRATEGY 9 ★ ★ ★

ESTABLISH PRIORITIES. Discipline is a routine followed with the total conviction of firmly established priorities. It requires a thinking process. Priorities help you know when you're not doing what you should be doing, like wasting time and energy on something that's counterproductive.

Discipline, Perseverance, and Aggressive Action

I want to take you inside a situation for a bit. Maybe you know some of this, but I want you to think about this situation from the vantage points of discipline, perseverance, and aggressive action. The story of Valley Forge is a story that should be seared into the mind of every American. It's who we are and where we come from. Once you understand and internalize the lessons of Valley Forge, you will never be the same.

In mid-December 1777, General George Washington led his Continental Army to Valley Forge following defeats at Philadelphia and Germantown. It was not a popular move. Some said he should have attacked the British at Philadelphia, or at least settled the Army in a town where they would be comfortable for the winter.

But Washington didn't want a comfortable army. He knew that armies never fight well coming out of cozy accommodations. He chose Valley Forge because of the training ground it would provide and its position vis-à-vis the British—close enough to observe them yet far enough away to preclude an enemy surprise. Plus, his position would deny the British valuable foraging area and protect the towns of Lancaster and Reading from attack. He also reasoned that he could supply his men from the rich stores of these communities.

His roughly 11,000 men certainly deserved a respite. They had fought hard throughout the year and were depleted in every way. The men were starving and cold, many without shoes. The trail into camp was blotched with blood. Four inches of snow fell on Christmas, with another four inches falling three days later.

The first job was to build shelter. Washington gave explicit guidance about how the log huts should be constructed and configured. It was a tall order. The men lacked tools, nails, and draft animals for hauling. Roofing was especially difficult to construct, so much so that Washington offered a substantial reward for the best solution to this vexing problem. It was more than a month before all the men were sheltered.

Some historians like to point out how crude and irregular these shelters turned out. I find it a senseless criticism. By developing a plan, and insisting on reasonable discipline, Washington ensured that his camp would adhere to the essentials of a military standard. The fact that his soldiers were unable to strictly conform to it was only a product of the horrible conditions under which they worked.

The men had virtually no food and subsisted on a diet of flour paste. Water was a problem. It had to be hauled up the steep hills in buckets from Valley Creek. Sanitation was primitive. Blankets were scarce, the men in rags. They often spent their nights beating themselves to ward off the cold.

Legs froze black, and men were carted off to hospitals to die or face amputation. Dysentery and smallpox were rampant. "Meat wagons" carted off the dead, stacked like cordwood. Over 3,000 Americans died.

It didn't have to be that way, but local suppliers sold food and matériel to the British for higher profits. Graft, ill fortune, and blind stupidity conspired against our brave soldiers. While politics and greed swirled around them, America's Army was forged in misery.

Meanwhile, in Philadelphia, the British Army lived the high life. Warm, well fed, and smartly uniformed in their red coats, they were the toast of the town. General Howe, the British commander, occupied himself with balls, galas, and his mistress, setting a personal example of indiscipline for his men to follow. The only reported downside was overcrowding in the local theaters. They were the perfect picture of an overconfident army gone soft. When informed that General Howe had captured Philadelphia, Benjamin Franklin replied, "I beg your pardon, sir, Philadelphia has captured General Howe."

Persevering at Valley Forge might have been story enough, but it was only a necessary sidelight to Washington's overall plan. Persevering wouldn't suffice. The Army needed to come out swinging in the spring. Somehow, the Continental Army would have to defeat the British in major engagements.

Washington was a superb leader, revered by his men. He was experienced in combat and an excellent strategist. To his credit, he also knew what he lacked—experience employing a large army against another large army. To this point most of his successes had been of the hit-and-run variety, irregular and inconclusive engagements where Howe had simply failed to press his advantage. Washington was looking for something more.

On Ben Franklin's recommendation, he brought in Baron Friedrich Wilhelm Ludolf Gerhard Augustin von Steuben—von Steuben for short. Von Steuben had a checkered past and a flair for the dramatic, but had served directly under Frederick the Great of Prussia, the greatest military schoolmaster of the time. Frederick taught that armies thrived on discipline and uniformity. His army fought in tightly formed units, maneuvering with great precision. He put an end to pillage and plundering and rewarded his soldiers with better pay, medical care, and decent living quarters. Most important, Friedrich preserved his army from slaughter, relying on surprise and maneuver to keep the enemy off balance.

Von Steuben learned his lessons well. Arriving at the camp in February, he was appalled by conditions there, but equally amazed at the spirit of the men. He correctly surmised that if such men could be taught the rudiments of large-unit tactics, they could become a formidable force. It was a difficult task, as Continental Army units came from different colonies and had different approaches to battle drill. Unlike European soldiers, who did what they were told, the Americans often asked, "Why?" But once they understood the logic of von Steuben's approach, they executed his commands with dedication and surprising energy.

Von Steuben's lesson plan is instructive. First, he handpicked a group of experienced combat veterans and formed a model platoon. He taught these men the proper stance, the position of attention: back erect, eyes forward, chest out. Then came the correct marching technique—begun with the left foot and maintained with a twenty-eight-inch stride. When marching was mastered, the men learned a synchronized twelve-step process of loading and firing their muskets. With complete competency achieved, these men became the drillmasters of the Army.

In a another month of hard work, the entire Army had learned the complexities of large-unit battle drill—oblique and column movements, sharp flanking movements, and the ability to change formations under simulated combat conditions. Washington stayed close to the process, honing his tactical skill and reinforcing the importance of the effort to his men.

Von Steuben was impressed. As the soldiers took pride in their newfound skills, morale soared—helped as well by the arrival of long-awaited supplies. As winter turned to spring, fresh recruits swelled the Army's numbers, each methodically inculcated with the new discipline. Brigades took turns on the parade fields, honing the precision of their maneuvers.

Later that spring the British Army abandoned Philadelphia—with Washington and the Continental Army in hot pursuit. They met in the Battle of Monmouth Courthouse, near Freehold, New Jersey. At the key moment of battle, Washington rode forward to rally his desperate men. He halted two retreating regiments and ordered them to stand firm and face the advancing enemy. They did so at great cost in casualties, buying Washington time to set up a defensive line on higher ground. As the British charged they not only faced the troops' musket fire, but Washington's artillery, now flanking them on both sides. The battle raged in hundred-degree heat.

The British brought up their own artillery and a deadly duel ensued. When an American artillery private was killed by British fire, his wife took his place at the cannon. Mary Ludwig Hayes, known to history as "Molly Pitcher," had been hauling water to the thirsty cannoneers when she answered the call to arms. Later in the day enemy cannon-shot would tear through the petticoat she was wearing, but she fought on, unscathed.

To von Steuben's satisfaction, Washington maneuvered his troops with great confidence, wheeling regiments under fire and into the line of combat. At the end of the battle the Americans counted their casualties at 69 dead and 116 wounded; British losses were estimated at 2,000, with numerous British deserters left straggling about the countryside.

Though the Battle of Monmouth Courthouse was not the decisive battle Washington sought, it set the tone for the ensuing campaign. Americans had persevered against great odds, learned a tremendous lesson in military discipline, and violently executed sophisticated battlefield tactics against a European foe.

The Legacy of Valley Forge

Many great Americans were "forged in the valley," among them Nathanael Greene and Alexander Hamilton. Because I'm from Ohio, my favorite is Anthony Wayne. You couldn't get through fifth-grade Ohio history without mastering the career nuances of "Mad Anthony." Not only did he survive Valley Forge, he led the advance element into the battle at Monmouth Courthouse. Wounded at Stony Point in 1779, he was a key leader at the siege of Yorktown—the final defeat of the British in the Revolutionary War.

In 1794, President George Washington called him out of retirement to lead the Legion of the United States against the British-supported Confederated Tribes. At the battle of Fallen Timbers, near my hometown of Toledo, Anthony Wayne succeeded where two other attempts had failed, and the Northwest Territory was opened for settlement. His victorious route from the battlefield is now U.S. Highway 24, known to Toledoans as "The Anthony Wayne Trail."

Valley Forge is the crucible of the American experience. It's where we proved our mettle. The United States Military was birthed there. It's where we as a nation discovered the ability to rally from adversity and emerge even stronger. It is truly sacred ground.

Yet most Americans have only a vague understanding of the price we paid there. Today Valley Forge is listed as one of the Ten Most Endangered

Parks by the National Parks Conservation Association. Unbelievably, buildings used by the Continental Army have fallen into disrepair, operating funds are in short supply, and projects are backlogged. What fitting irony for a culture plagued with the scourge of indiscipline.

But the beauty here is that as the culture puts more stock in license, in the "I'm free to do whatever I want, whenever I want" mentality, the value of discipline increases—because it's so rare. It's like gold. What Washington and von Steuben considered of primary importance is avoided at all costs today. But for those willing to sacrifice and commit, discipline still yields the big dividends.

★ ★ ★ STRATEGY 10 ★ ★ ★

MAKE DISCIPLINE A HABIT. Discipline has to become a habit. Consistency is the key. We know that every discipline affects every other discipline. The habits build on one another and become mutually reinforcing. The devil is in the details, so pay a lot of attention to details. The good news is that solid habits eventually become second nature, a series of actions leading to enhanced performance. Ultimately, discipline allows and facilitates freedom.

The Discipline Habit

Practiced discipline becomes a habit. In fact, that's what discipline is—a series of actions. It's consistency. The habits build on one another and become mutually reinforcing. The yield is enhanced performance. Indiscipline is just the opposite—it's a series of bad habits, consistently making bad choices at the slightest temptation. You can develop good habits or bad habits. Simple as that.

As we say in the military, "Discipline is a readiness issue." If the force isn't disciplined, we're not ready for combat. And we've got to be ready.

We look at various indicators to gauge our readiness. The indicators tell us how well we're motivating and focusing our soldiers. The number of screwups is a pretty good indicator of how disciplined a force we've developed. Accidents, injuries, and the crime rate tell the tale. When the trends are negative, we lock things down until we're back in the discipline groove.

Discipline is a routine followed with the conviction of firmly established priorities. It requires a thinking process—you have to know when you're not doing what you should be doing, like wasting time and energy on something that's counterproductive. Good habits begin with conscious decisions and, with practice, are turned over to the unconscious mind. Solid habits eventually become second nature, like the ease with which you brush your teeth. Consistency is the key.

You can reinforce self-discipline success with small rewards—up to a point. But you also have to buy into delayed gratification; by being tough on yourself now, you'll reap greater rewards down the road. Eye on the prize. Toughing it out. Eventually the habits become ingrained.

You're assisted in this effort by the undeniable power of your unconscious mind. For every single brain cell thinking conscious thoughts, there are 10 million cells doing other things. The unconscious mind regulates your body, stores acquired memories and information, and maintains your habits. Once you decide what these habits will be, you ingrain them through practice, and put the dynamic power of your unconscious mind to work.

As you develop discipline, you gain control of your mind and environment. You get out ahead of life and arrange things to support the goals you want to accomplish. If you're working to become physically fit, you watch how you stock your refrigerator. If you're working for all A's, you learn to manage distractions like TV and video games. Salespeople learn to manage their time like a racing team's pit crew, quickly refueling to get back on the track.

Arrange your environment to support your goals.

Washington didn't want the Army in a town for the winter getting soft. He chose the more challenging route to success.

Arrange life so there's always something directly in front of you to keep you moving forward. Be tough on yourself, so you're ready when the going gets tough. Even the little things count. Discipline is a series of little things done correctly. That's why von Steuben started with a soldier's posture, something we still do today.

Washington. Von Steuben. Molly Pitcher. Mad Anthony Wayne. Just four of the thousands of who came out swinging from Valley Forge. We are the descendants of their great effort. We carry the seed of their vision. This country isn't made of sugar candy—and neither are you.

Train Tough Challenge

List three areas where you need more discipline.

1. _____

2. _____

3. _____

What are you going to do about it?

_____

_____

_____

3

———★———

CONFIDENCE

The Ultimate Lifestyle

I don't deny that I was damned good. If there is such a thing as "the best," I was at least one of the title contenders. I had a full life and enjoyed just about every minute of it because that's how I lived.
—General Chuck Yeager, U.S. Air Force

For several years I didn't feel comfortable around Galen McPherson. We were stuck in a Clint Eastwood movie, facing off in the church foyer with that eerie whistling in the background, each waiting for the other guy to draw.

We were like two women who show up at a party in the same dress. There's that chill in the air. You can hear the wheels turning, "Who's perkiest? Who's best preserved? How soon can we get out of here?"

But there was no point in creating a scene in the church lobby. We stayed out of each other's way. He worked on his committees and I worked on mine. We had an unspoken agreement to proceed in parallel universes.

Comparisons are counterproductive, but sometimes we just can't seem to help ourselves. It's usually not the dog ahead or behind but the cur next to us that rubs us the wrong way.

That was Galen and me.

Then one Sunday in the church parking lot Galen opened the trunk of his car and pulled out a rifle. At first I thought he was going to shoot me with it. "Here take this," he said, "I don't use it much anymore, I'd like you to have it. Maybe you and your son can have some fun with it."

I don't know if it's the Christian thing to do to give a guy a rifle in the church parking lot, but it definitely broke the ice. We went from alpha male syndrome right into male bonding. It's amazing what the transfer of an implement of destruction can accomplish.

Anyway, I started learning more about my new friend Galen.

Galen was raised in a culture far different than mine—the U.S. Air Force. He was an Air Force Academy graduate and a former fighter pilot. We were from opposite poles of the U.S. Military universe. He interpreted my Army bearing and attention to detail as arrogant and anal; I interpreted his swagger and self-confidence as overbearing and haughty. Turns out we were both right.

Galen does have oodles of confidence, but at the Air Force Academy, installing confidence is part of the job. Officers have a "fundamental moral obligation to the persons they lead to strike a tone of confidence." It's on their Web site. You can look it up. The academy sees confidence as a moral obligation.

Fighter pilot training seals the deal.

Galen flew the F4 Phantom, the last of the brute force fighters in which moving the stick directly controlled the aircraft. Now, of course, it's all electronic.

Galen actually thought he could outfight F14s, 15s, 16s, and 18s in a plane with thirty-year-old technology. He often succeeded.

"There is a fighter pilot mentality," he told me, "there's no second place in a dogfight, just a winner and a dead guy. Fair is dead, so in combat you stack the deck."

Stacking the deck includes realistic training to shorten the learning cycle. Flight simulators provide repetitive learning with controlled risk. Two-hour debriefings on a forty-minute mission are the norm.

Most important, confidence is developed and strengthened at every turn. The Air Force instills confidence through a number of small successes that ultimately produce a trained, confident, and high-performing pilot. Pilots walk, talk, and act with self-assurance and confidence.

"You're trained to think you're the best pilot in the room," says Galen, "but also to consider that everyone else in the room thinks the same thing. It's a paradox, but ultimately we hunt in packs and work as a team, so you also develop confidence in the guys on your wing."

Air Force training is designed to turn pilots into winners, empowered and prepared for any contingency. It's a finely honed, confidence-producing system.

Galen McPherson is now a business analyst with MSX International. In the Air Force he had overseas assignments in England and Korea; with MSX he's had stints in Germany, Italy, Japan, and Dubai. He's the guy they send in early to see if a process is doable and if there's profit for both MSX and the client. Like a fighter pilot, he uses pattern recognition, doing a quick scan to size up the situation.

"Situational awareness is critical," Galen told me. "In a fighter you're functioning in 3D, aware of where you are in time and space, where the enemy is and what the mission is. When I hit the ground to analyze a company the feeling is very much the same. I want to know where it is and where it's going."

I'm sure he does it all with a great deal of confidence—he's a great guy.

The Primacy of Confidence

The military taught me to carry 3- by 5-inch cards to take notes on during the day. I now have several feet of 3 by 5 cards full of helpful quotes and great ideas. Here's one of them. It's something Mary Matalin said her father told her—"Only one thing separates successful people from unsuccessful people. It isn't money or brains. It's confidence. And what creates confidence is three things: being prepared, having experience, and never giving up."

Wow.

So it's *not* money; it's *not* brains—it's *confidence.*

Think about that for a minute.

Not money. Now there's a powerful idea.

Not brains. How many brainiacs still miss the point entirely?

It's confidence! The ultimate lifestyle. That's what separates the successful from the unsuccessful.

There are all manner of people who started out with little or no money, with perfectly normal IQs, who have nevertheless parlayed modest gifts into success. The separation is made possible with confidence.

And what creates confidence?

Preparation. Experience. Tenacity.

Let's start with *tenacity,* because without it you're not going anywhere. The world is not going to roll over and play dead just because you're in the game. No, the world is going to knock you on your butt over and over again. Sorry, but we all know that's the way it is. You can't just lie there. You have to get up, over and over again. You have to learn to thrive on adversity, allowing yourself the freedom to "fail forward faster."

You'll need the *knowledge* of how to get back up. But you gain the knowledge only by getting knocked down in the first place. So you have to be out there taking the hits. Dealing with pain. Getting back up and trying again. Gaining experience. That way, you build confidence one step at a time.

Preparation is also critical. The Air Force doesn't take pilot candidates out on the runway and say, "You'll figure it out. Good luck."

No. They take them through an iterative process, building confidence through baby steps that cumulatively create trained fighter pilots. The failures take place in the simulator, where errors can be corrected and successes reinforced. Confidence builds one step at a time, through a system of trained recovery.

You actually have to train yourself to recover. And that's not easy.

You need a big friend on your side—Desire. Desire fuels the entire process.

Desire is how guys become fighter pilots. There's never a shortage of guys who want to hurtle through the air at outrageous speeds while optimizing the latest technology. The Air Force doesn't have to pull teeth for volunteers. They're standing in line.

These guys have the desire. Being strapped in, or upside down, or really, really dizzy is not a big deal to these guys because becoming a fighter pilot is more important than temporary discomfort. They're willing to leap hurdles and squeeze through wickets because of that desire. They're guys focusing on their potential, not their limitations. And when I say guys I mean gals too, obviously.

★ ★ ★ **STRATEGY 11** ★ ★ ★

UNDERSTAND THE COMPONENTS OF CONFIDENCE. Confidence is the result of preparation, experience, and tenacity. Preparation is a combination of hard work and the mental effort of planning. Tenacity is the mentality that thrives on adversity, made possible through a trained system of recovery. Confidence comes with experience—especially the experience of overcoming adversity. Desire fuels the process.

The ones who make it have "the right stuff," as Chuck Yeager liked to say. They earn their wings through preparation, experience, and the tenacity to persevere.

That's confidence.

Competence—Jet Engine of Confidence

It's hard to develop confidence on the cheap.

I know. Like most people, I've tried the shortcuts. Faking it might work for a while, but there's no substitute for actually knowing what you're doing. It's called *competence*.

Competence is the jet engine of confidence. Without the engine, all you have is a good-looking airplane that doesn't fly.

Let me put it this way, if competence is an issue, as it is for a lot of people, you're probably in the wrong business. If you like what you're doing and feel as though you're responding to a calling, then competence pretty much slides into place. You naturally want to master the nuances of competence, all the way to excellence.

On the other hand many people wind up in careers they're really not all that interested in. For them learning is a drag.

I know, straight up, I never wanted to become a fighter pilot. Sure I saw the glamour, but glamour alone would not have taken me through the rigors of pilot training. I don't like getting dizzy. Period. I don't even go on most of the rides at an amusement park. Technology is not a big turn-on for me. Even hot cars have only a marginal effect. I do like to shoot things, but I've always found plenty of ways to do that on the ground. The wild blue yonder is something I can live without.

I lack the right stuff to become a fighter pilot. And I'm OK with that. Really.

The beauty of military service is that there's something for just about everybody—literally hundreds of specialties from which to choose. Some are in greater demand than others, but there's always a wide choice. There's no excuse for not finding something you like.

Life outside the military offers even more choices. The key is to find something you like doing, something you want to do well. Devote yourself to your gift. Our subconscious responds most positively when we're working in our true calling, dedicating ourselves to getting it right.

Competence does not come easily; it requires preparation and experience. Preparation implies strategic design—a plan for improved performance—and then a learning environment for acquiring skills. Finally, competence requires practical experience, ideally in situations of increasing challenge and difficulty that demonstrate competence—and increase confidence.

Become competent and you'll become confident. *Confidence* is 60 percent the same word as *competence*. They even sound the same.

★ ★ ★ **STRATEGY 12** ★ ★ ★

BUILD CONFIDENCE THROUGH COMPETENCE. We're confident about what we do well. We learn best what we enjoy. *Confidence* and *competence* are 60 percent the same word—they're inextricably linked. Once you understand and accept that link, you're going to be tremendously more effective—and confident.

Build a Case for Yourself

Beyond the foundations of confidence—preparation, experience, tenacity—strategic design is critical. We want to systematically build confidence. The question is, how do we convince ourselves that we're worthy of self-confidence?

The answer is to build a case for yourself.

Seriously. Forget self-criticism and use positive self-talk to build a case, just as you would if you were taking your case to a jury.

What are your strong points?

Do you believe in who you are and what you are doing?

Have you done the work?

What have you accomplished already?

Again, keep it positive.

Who's supporting you? Who's in your wolf pack?

Think of your group as an elite unit. We find in the U.S. Military that elite units generally outperform their more vanilla counterparts. Marines, Navy Seals, Green Berets, Rangers, and Airborne units all carry a special pride and confidence that comes with being part of an elite team.

Build a case for yourself. Find reasons for confidence.

Then act *as if* . . .

Act *as if* things are going to go your way, as if you can persevere regardless of the situation.

Take a look at posture.

How do matadors stand? How do they walk?

I'm not saying you want to strut around acting arrogant, but stance and demeanor give matadors confidence—a confidence they communicate to the bull and the crowd. Most important, the matadors themselves feel it.

We apply the same logic with new recruits. The first thing we correct is their posture. When we straighten them up, their confidence improves. Everything we do builds from that initial instruction, and everything we do is designed to build confidence.

Build confidence one step at a time, no matter your starting point. Make a case for yourself.

Ultimately, confidence is a lifestyle choice. You either install it in your mind-set, or you don't.

Everything we do is a reflection of confidence—attitudes, goals, and accomplishments.

Think big.

Build a case for yourself.

Train Tough Challenge

Build a case for yourself. List three reasons you can persevere in any situation:

1. _____

2. _____

3. _____

4

---★---

SACRIFICE

Sorry, You Really *Can't* Have It All

Bob . . . I want you to take Buna, or not come back alive.
General Douglas MacArthur to General Robert Eichelberger

Bob Eichelberger was the commandant at West Point when the Japanese attacked Pearl Harbor. In a speech three days before, he had predicted the attack. Conspiracy theorists still speculate he must have been in the know. But Eichelberger just knew the Japanese, having made a personal study of them. He was 55 at the time, but that didn't stop him from requesting immediate assignment to a combat unit.

Eichelberger served the Army at a time when promotions were slow and the pay lousy; still, he never seriously considered doing anything else. Not that he couldn't have. He was a smart guy. When Eisenhower finished first in his class at the highly competitive Leavenworth School, Eichelberger was only a few points behind. They were deskmates at the school, by virtue of the alphabetic arrangement of students, and they became friends. They also shared a common pal, George S. Patton, who was a few years ahead of them careerwise, and a ball of flame they could look to for inspiration.

Many thought Eichelberger was too preoccupied with West Point football, a program that had long been a doormat for East Coast teams. He fought to allow bigger players into the school, and hired a professional coaching staff. Bob Eichelberger didn't like to lose. "In combat warfare there may be no game next week," he later wrote.

And combat warfare was where Eichelberger was heading. Originally on his way to Australia to oversee training, General MacArthur shanghaied him instead for the Buna operation.

Buna sits on the northeast end of New Guinea. The area held by the enemy was small, but important. Buna was a linchpin for the Japanese goal of isolating Australia and New Zealand and cutting off supply lines to the United States—all part of their plan to dominate Asia.

Eichelberger received his orders on November 30, 1942, joining a battle that was two weeks old. What he found was a nightmare that would haunt him the rest of his life.

The Americans and Australians were attacking out of a swamp, their exit blocked by mountains. The Japanese were dug in on dry land along the coast, with ample roads to relocate forces and meet attacks.

U.S. forces were a shambles. The jungle had taken a terrible toll. Malaria, dysentery, and jungle rot were rampant; virtually every soldier was sick with fever. Many were raw recruits originally programmed for the war in Europe, unprepared for jungle warfare. Fetid water, snakes, crocodiles, vegetation so thick it had to be hacked through, and constant rain mired their efforts.

They existed at the end of a long supply line—on one-third rations. With their uniforms in tatters and worn-out shoes, discipline weakened and leadership faltered. Japanese sniping and ambush ruled the day. The Americans had a single artillery piece to employ. In many places the Japanese numbered ten times estimates—in all, 12,000 strong. The U.S. efforts bogged down; planned attacks petered out at the first difficulty.

Yet they had no choice but to go forward. Remaining in the mosquito-infested swamp would only increase the scourge of malaria among the already weakened force.

Eichelberger faced a daunting task. After briefings from his staff, he ventured forward to the front lines. He found the situation even worse than the staff had let on. Units were intermingled and had poor communication. Knowledge of Japanese positions was negligible, and moving about often required wading in hip-high swamp water. Tremendous time and effort were required to carry wounded to the rear.

A week after receiving his marching orders from MacArthur, Eichelberger found himself personally engaged with the enemy. When a U.S. attack stalled, Eichelberger left his observation post and went forward, leading the way. Though against regulations at the time, Eichelberger continued to wear his three-star insignia, hoping to inspire his men.

He remembered well his mission—"Take Buna, or don't come back alive."

Beyond taking the personal risk that the situation demanded, Eichelberger directed immediate changes. He delegated the supply problem to the capable hands of Colonel George De Graaf. Soon ammunition and rations were moving freely, and the men received hot meals whenever possible. Officers too burned out to continue the fight were replaced, and unit integrity was reestablished and communication improved.

Still, the situation remained precarious. On Christmas Eve Day, two Americans took actions that would lead to the posthumous awarding of Medals of Honor. Sergeant Elmer J. Burr threw himself on an enemy grenade to save the life of his company commander, and Sergeant Kenneth E. Gruennert courageously led attacks on two Japanese pillboxes while severely wounded.

Christmas dawned with a Japanese air bombardment. Spirits were low. Evidence of Santa Claus was nowhere to be found. General Eichelberger's Christmas dinner consisted of a cup of soup. He would lose 30 pounds in his first month of combat.

Siege warfare to destroy a well-disciplined, entrenched enemy is always the worst kind of fight. At times the battle seemed lost, but American courage and stubbornness won out. In the end, American troops accomplished the impossible: crossing an "unfordable" stream, under fire, at night.

Most of the enemy chose to die rather than surrender, and they died at a prodigious rate. Final Japanese attacks took place along the shore, with U.S. machine guns cutting them down, their bodies left to roll with the tide. The site came to be known as Maggot Beach.

Three U.S. general officers were wounded by enemy fire; 586 brave Americans lost their lives. By January 3, 1943, organized resistance ceased, the battle won.

The fight at Buna came before napalm, effective flamethrowers, and air superiority, at a time when stiff resistance couldn't be bypassed, but had to be confronted. Buna offered some of the worst conditions of the war. Even at Guadalcanal, as bad as it was, U.S. forces held dry ground and kept the Japanese in the jungle; at Buna, it was the other way around.

Buna was the first time the U.S. Army defeated the Japanese in a major ground engagement in World War II. But it came at a price.

★ ★ ★   **STRATEGY 13**   ★ ★ ★

COMMIT. Your level of commitment is measured by sacrifice—the two go hand in hand. You can't walk off the field when you're committed; you accept a certain amount of pain, even fear. That's why, as human beings, one of our most treasured attributes is the ability to sacrifice. When we're committed, distractors lose their power. Our focus is on moving forward.

Sacrifice: The Cost of Doing Business

There's a cost of doing business. *Sacrifice.*

Every lesson learned comes with a price.

The price paid at Buna is beyond comprehension. Every one of those men left the safety of life in the United States and traveled halfway around the world—to fight in a living hell. For every American killed more than three were wounded. The vast majority fought on even when they were sick with fever. It was an effort demanding the utmost sacrifice.

Many lessons were learned at the battle for Buna, among them the importance of communication, leadership, and air power. We learned that Japanese strategies and tactics were inflexible and not terribly creative. Had they abandoned their enclave mentality and done more counterattacking, the outcome at Buna might have been much different.

Most important, we learned that under relentless pressure, the Japanese would crack like any other army. They weren't ten feet tall. Determined Americans, under inspired leadership, would be equal to the task.

Though General Eichelberger's personal sacrifice is well chronicled, it's only one example of what soldiers sacrificed during the operation.

Sacrifice is one of the most important secrets of the United States Military. It's ingrained in everything we do. It's the foundation stone of our values. At the moment we raise our right hand to take the oath of service we know we're entering a new world, a world with a different value system. It's an act of courage. A leap into the unknown. And every member of the armed forces takes that step alone. You take that step hoping for the best, but deep down you know you're spinning the roulette wheel of sacrifice—and you never know what you'll be asked to give.

I raised my right hand in January 1971. It was a John Wayne moment, one of those times you suck in some air and do what feels right.

It was hard. The Vietnam War was in progress, an event that began when I was in the sixth grade. Like all the kids of my generation, the war would dog our hopes and dreams throughout our formative years. Despite what the counterculture was saying, I sensed right away that I was joining a great team.

My military instructors were more focused than my college professors. There was an urgency to what they taught, knowing they might be sending us to the battlefield. It wasn't "learn French because someday you'll want to visit Paris," it was "learn this now and it might save your life."

They taught me that every worthwhile endeavor requires sacrifice. Sometimes the sacrifice seems small and mundane, but it still makes a difference.

Fifteen years later, I made it a personal goal to graduate first in my class at the Army's Command and General Staff College. There were about 1,000 officers enrolled, so it was a tall order. It wasn't long before I realized I was going to have to give up some things in order to achieve my goal. Golf and TV had to go.

I was playing a lot of golf at the time, so for a while it seemed like a real sacrifice. But when I considered the cost in time and energy that golf demanded, it became obvious it had to go. I stayed active athletically, but golf was out.

Same with TV. There was no way I could be whiling away hours in front of the boob tube and bust top grades at the same time. If there was a football or basketball game I wanted to watch, I'd tune in for the fourth quarter. I'd watch only the final innings of a baseball game. Most of the drama comes at the end anyway. So I sacrificed a couple things in pursuit of my goal.

I didn't sacrifice family time. I stayed involved there and found some innovative ways to incorporate study with my kids' various activities.

To this day I don't play much golf. For me, it's too consuming. I know several guys who are avid golfers who cram it into their schedules and still manage to get their work done. For me it doesn't work.

The point is that none of us can do it all. Some things have to go. Some things have to be sacrificed. I didn't graduate first in my class, but I did accomplish a lot more than if I hadn't tried. I learned again the value of sacrifice.

★ ★ ★ **STRATEGY 14** ★ ★ ★

CHOOSE SACRIFICE OVER SHORTCUTS. There's always a shortcut. Always. And let's face it, we all take the shortcut from time to time. The shortcut is the easier choice. But there are some situations where you must choose sacrifice in order to be effective. Sacrifice is uncomfortable; you have to see it as a cost of doing business. Because it's often counterintuitive, you have to consciously and rationally determine to make sacrifices.

Strange Lessons in Sacrifice

The concept of sacrifice is not entirely rational, which makes it an uncomfortable subject for a lot of people. In our increasingly self-centered culture, giving your life for your country is counterintuitive. Sacrificing anything has become uncomfortable. We want it all.

Yet sacrifice is deeply embedded in the human psyche. Most of the world's religions include the ritual of sacrifice, either to appease the gods or to atone for guilt. On a very primal level we sense that in order to get, we have to give.

Great leaders know this.

General George Patton probably never said what was attributed to him in the movie *Patton,* that bit about "not dying for your country, but getting the other fellow to die for his." Patton didn't coddle his troops by telling them to keep their heads down or to not take chances. He knew that victory came with a price. What he actually said was, "Some of us are going to die, but we are tough enough to take a dozen of the enemy before we go."

If you're trying to get by without sacrifice, you're making a mistake.

We often look at other, more successful people and see only the glory, forgetting what they had to give up to get there. We rationalize the success of others by focusing on their wealth, pedigree, or natural ability.

But the truth is, it takes a lot of work to make it look easy.

Part of our problem is that we see a lot of dirt balls having major success. We throw our hands up in despair instead of analyzing how they're doing it. If you do your own analysis, you'll find that most of these people have actually taken very traditional routes to the top in spite of themselves: Mike Tyson, Eminem, Madonna. The story is always the same—talent and a new spin followed by hard work and sacrifice.

You'd probably think a guy like me wouldn't have much respect for a guy like Dennis Rodman, for instance.

You'd be wrong.

You see, I learned a lot about Dennis Rodman while I was researching *Trial By Basketball*. Yes, Dennis has a lot of problems. He's a lousy role model. He'd never make it in the military. But in focusing on his downside, we forget about the sacrifices Dennis Rodman made to succeed in a sport that puts a premium on all the attributes he flaunts. He often looks like a clown, acts like a clown, and, to the untrained, appears to be a clown. But the reality is somewhat different.

Dennis Rodman taught himself to be one of the most effective role players ever to play the game of basketball. He essentially gave up shooting to concentrate on defense and rebounding. He developed to the point where he could shut down high-scoring players much bigger than him, and became a record-breaking rebounder. He maintained a relentless physical training program that perfected his already awesome physical abilities. Realizing he would be a primary foul target late in key games, he trained himself to become a clutch free-throw shooter.

Yes, watching Dennis Rodman was painful. Yes, he could have accomplished much more with the personal discipline to corral his eccentricities and blind stupidity. But five NBA Championship rings ain't bad. Sacrifice is probably not a word in his vocabulary, but it's a major part of his success.

Whether you're a successful den mother or Madonna, sacrifice is part of the mix.

I apologize to the purists for putting George Patton and Dennis Rodman in the same section, but in unique ways their lives speak to us on the importance of sacrifice.

★ ★ ★ **STRATEGY 15** ★ ★ ★

CHOOSE "ANYTHING" OVER "EVERYTHING." You can have anything you want, but not everything. Sacrifice is the operative concept here. Put a value on things, blowing ballast in order to achieve what's really important to you. Sacrifice is what makes "anything" possible.

Anything Versus Everything

A few months ago my wife Heidi and I visited Sun City Anthem in Henderson, Nevada. It's truly a remarkable development that offers state-of-the-art housing options in a beautiful, natural setting.

Each morning, for three mornings, we visited the flagship mansion, and each time we beat the crowd and had the place to ourselves. For a little while we lived lifestyles of the rich and famous. Heidi loved all the amenities of the house, but it was the view that blew my mind. The place had a patio with a swimming pool built into the side of the mountain, edging on a cliff. Golfers practiced their craft in a lush green valley below. Las Vegas loomed in the distance. It was breathtaking.

On the first morning I said to my wife "You know, I think I can see the benefit of making a ton of money and living in a place like this."

The silence was deafening. At the time I was working a book idea, with no advance and limited prospects of success. I deeply felt that it was my calling, but it required sacrifice. Being in that house brought home just how much sacrifice—and in a rather painful way.

The second morning was windy and cold, and the view from the patio was less spectacular.

By the third morning I was cured. Even Heidi seemed less enamored. And she had stopped hitting me.

We realized that we had made other choices in our lives, that we had willingly passed on some things. The lure of materialism is powerful, but some things are more important. A good dose of sour grapes was helpful too; swimming pools require a lot of maintenance.

Whatever it takes.

You've got to do whatever it takes to stay focused on your goals.

You can have anything you want in life, you just can't have everything. You're going to have to choose. You're going to have to draw on one of the tried-and-true attributes that we hold so dear in the U.S. Military—sacrifice.

As they say in the Navy, blow ballast. If you want to make top speed toward your goals, the deadweight has to go. You're not going to reach your destination on the party barge. Sacrifice builds on discipline, often on the discipline to temporarily or permanently deny yourself certain pleasures or courses of action. Nobody can do it all. Nobody can have it all.

Pushing yourself may not make for a particularly balanced life. Consecrating yourself to a mission requires intense concentration, and the setting aside of distractions. A warrior on a quest is a different person than someone out for a good time.

Warriors plan their mission in finite detail. They prepare and prioritize. They ensure their support base is secure. They decide what's important and what must be given up. They determine their level of commitment and what the sacrifice will be. They consciously decide what to sacrifice—and they move out.

Train Tough Challenge

List two areas where you're willing to sacrifice.

1. _____

2. _____

PART TWO

———— ★ ————

THE BUSINESS OF THE UNITED STATES MILITARY

It's a dangerous business.
We do it well. Here's how.

5

———★———

ENDSTATE

Understanding the Mission

American Naval Forces provide a powerful yet unobtrusive presence; strategic deterrence; control of the seas; extended and continuous on-scene crisis response; project precise power from the sea; and provide sealift if larger scale scenarios emerge.

U.S. Navy Vision Statement

M otivation. Discipline. Confidence. Sacrifice. You're going to need all four just to get through this chapter.

This is going to be hard. This is what we call *officer business.* The stuff we start teaching officers when they're cadets, that we drill into them in their basic and advanced courses, the Command and General Staff Colleges, and the War Colleges. If they're lucky, these processes still plague them as generals.

It's hard.

It's called figuring out what we're doing.

A simple concept, yet how many of us stumble around in our own lives and complain about the lack of direction in our businesses and organizations?

It's easier to do the same old thing every day . . . for a while. A lot of people don't want to know. They figure it'll all work out in the end, and sometimes it does.

But that's a dangerous attitude in the military. Our wake-up calls are very painful.

We want to make sure we're doing the right job—and doing it right.

I'm going to give you a thumbnail sketch of how we think in the United States Military, a little bit of our intellectual process. Believe me, it's going to hurt me as much as it hurts you.

But if you'll hang in there, I think you'll see how you can apply this process to your business, your organization, and your personal life.

I'm going to keep things Bender simple. We'll stay out of the weeds. I want you to see the thinking process, and be supple enough to apply it to your own situation as we go along.

Later, you can use this chapter as a reference.

But no wimping out!

American History 101

It's imperative that American fighting men and women understand their role in history. The same should be true for the American citizen. It's hard to know where you're going if you don't know where you've been.

Let's talk about the United States of America.

Who are we, really? What makes us unique?

What are our principles? What do we value?

Our history provides many of the answers. You had a bunch of wayfarers who left Europe, a land of kings, queens, and nobility who ruled through a system of monarchy and aristocracy. The system told the people how to worship, and persecuted those who deviated. The persecution was sometimes physical, but it was also economic. It was hard to earn a living when you were shunned. It was hard to go on living with no voice to be heard, and no stake in the system.

So they left.

These dear people valued freedom, justice, and democracy. They attempted to build a culture based on freedom, honesty, and the common good. They valued hard work and a system of free enterprise to capitalize on the bounty they found in America. Part of the reason they did such a great job is that leaders emerged who could articulate principles, values, and a vision. A free press helped people access the ideas and events of the time.

Slavery created another subset of Americans who shared similar values—freedom, justice, and a voice in the system. African Americans shared the same vision, but traveled an even tougher road.

The American journey has been paid with a price, and sometimes challenged with moral ambiguity. The same energy that led us here in the first place pushed us west, encroaching deeper and deeper into the lands of Native Americans. We fought them, too. Their choices were difficult, and although they fought bravely, their strategies and fighting capabilities were no match for the new Americans. I'm not sure we've totally come to grips with this chapter in our history.

We kept the European powers out of our backyard. We declared our independence. We fought with the British and Spanish and later the Germans and the Japanese in the world wars. We went eyeball to eyeball with the Soviet Union for fifty years.

Our military history is a proud one, though not without its failures. We have generally misjudged threats, and sometimes been ill prepared to meet them. For a long time the oceans helped to protect us. The American soldier has always defended our country, sometimes paying the price for our unpreparedness in blood.

Yes, we have a proud history, but we've got to do better.

We need a vision of our country, and the world, that we can all get behind, that will guide us to the next level.

That Vision Thing

President George Bush the First served his country as a Navy pilot in World War II and then ably in a series of public service positions throughout his distinguished career. He was a great commander in chief during Desert Storm.

But to his ultimate detriment he pooh-poohed the vision thing. Maybe he spent so much time in government, mastering the art of management, that he lost sight of where America was going.

Americans don't like it when that happens. We've never been content with just muddling through, managing crises as they occur. We look for energy in our leaders, leaders with a vision of what our country can be, that "Shining City on a Hill" with shared bounty, security, stability, and the sense we're harnessing our assets to move forward.

President John F. Kennedy provided vision with his goal of a "man on the moon by the end of the decade." It was a goal that was forward-looking and energizing. It symbolized our desire to keep exploring, expand the frontier, and harness technology to improve the quality of our lives.

Vision is a mental picture, an ideal endstate. It's a specific destination, with an underlying sense of purpose, something that springs from our principles and values. It's not just what we *don't* want, it's what we *really* want.

★ ★ ★   **STRATEGY 16**   ★ ★ ★

HAVE A VISION. Get a picture in your mind of an ideal endstate. Vision is a specific destination, something that springs from your principles and what you truly value. It's not what you *don't* want, it's what you *really* want. By definition, your quest implies a destination, and that destination is determined by vision.

Strategy—And the Art of Strategic Design

Let's use U.S. foreign policy to see how strategy is tied to the national vision. Although the line between foreign and domestic policy becomes more blurred all the time, we'll try to stay out of domestic politics because the U.S. Military really doesn't play a role there. It's also rather messy.

One of the nice things about the military's role is that, despite changes in administrations, our role in the national strategy isn't altered. American principles and values run deep, and the vision is clear. It's bigger than a single president and his administration or a political party. Sure, the emphasis changes, but the vision is constant.

The United States seeks to promote democracy and free trade. That's it in a nutshell. But these are two very important goals.

Promoting democracy is key to both our security and the well-being of planet Earth. Democracies don't often fight each other, and they make far better decisions. A planet comprised of democracies would be a better place. More stable, more secure.

Free trade is also important. Nations that trade with each other tend to get along better. The whole process of international trade opens doors—and minds. The "business of America is business," and our domestic economy is very much tied to global economic growth. A rising tide raises all boats.

In order for democracies to flourish and economies to grow, security and stability are essential. That's the role of the U.S. Military. And it can be a dangerous role. In our quest for stability and security, we sometimes inhibit the natural growing pains that developing nations experience as they move toward democracy. Finding the balance requires enlightened leadership—and a grand strategy.

Grand strategy is the master plan for reaching our goals, using the available means.

The "means" are like power tools, and America has a shed full.

We have tremendous economic power, and with it the capability to help others, to choose trading partners, and even to boycott nations when necessary.

We have tremendous diplomatic power. Since the end of World War II the world has looked to America for leadership, including moral leadership. The United Nations is located here; our embassies span the globe.

Finally, we have become the world's premier military power, with the ability to project power around the world.

These are the means by which the United States carries out our strategy—economic, diplomatic, and military.

★ ★ ★ STRATEGY 17 ★ ★ ★

MASTER THE ART OF STRATEGIC DESIGN. Will you use a direct or indirect approach? What is your center of gravity? What are the decisive points of your mission? Its culminating point? What is your exit strategy?

The Military Piece

The military piece of America's overall strategy is called the National Security Strategy. The president signs off on it.

It speaks to how we'll enhance our overall security and maintain the strongest possible defense capability. It's a great document because it gets everybody in the military on the same page.

Our first job is to deter aggression. To do this we want to maintain a credible overseas presence, which demonstrates commitment to our allies and allows us to train with them, coordinate planning, and share intelligence.

Combating terrorism has moved up in the pecking order. We know now that we'll be asked to strike terrorist bases and the rogue nations that sponsor them. Stopping the spread of weapons of mass destruction has taken on a new urgency in the face of state-sponsored terrorism. We've upped our efforts to prevent the use of such weapons and to protect ourselves against their effects.

Our forces must also be ready to participate in peacekeeping and peace enforcement operations.

We support the war on drugs.

Finally, we must to be ready for war in space, meaning that we want to maintain free access and maintain our position as the world's premier space power. We want to deter threats to U.S. interests in space and prevent the use of space for weapons of mass destruction. It's not as far out as it seems; in fact, the U.S. Army just activated the First Space Brigade.

How and when to employ U.S. military forces is also a part of the National Security Strategy. We try to categorize national interests as either vital, important, or humanitarian. We know we can't do it all; we also have to factor in the cost-benefit analysis. What are the stakes? What are the prospects of success? What are the costs, both human and financial, of engaging the task?

We want our troops going forward with a clear mission. Insofar as is possible, we want the support of our friends and allies—and the American public. Once we commit, we will pursue our objective with unwavering commitment.

That's the National Security Strategy. You can see how it supports America's Grand Strategy, which is to promote democracy and free trade around the world.

But there's more.

There's a subset of the National Security Strategy called the *Joint Strategic Planning Document.* This document, prepared under the auspices of the Joint Chiefs of Staff, attempts to ascertain the various risks inherent in the world environment, identify objectives, and assess the resources available to do the job. It also identifies the strategic concepts, or military strategy, for getting the job done.

Our senior military leaders rely on time-tested concepts to help define a military strategy. These military strategic concepts extend through the operational level of war, ultimately influencing the way battles are fought at the tactical level. You can take these military concepts and see how we applied them in Gulf War II. With a few modifications, you can also apply them to your personal and business endeavors.

Military strategy is built on the following concepts:

Centers of Gravity. What is the major factor from which each side derives its freedom of action, physical strength, or will to fight? We want to focus our main effort against the enemy's primary source of power, which he will undoubtedly seek to protect. It could be his capital, his navy, or the will of his people. In an alliance it may be the defeat of a key country. By focusing on our enemy's center of gravity, we create a deteriorating effect in our enemy's efforts, one that will impact his morale, cohesion, and will to fight. Of course, the dagger cuts both ways. One school of thought maintains the center of gravity in the Vietnam War was U.S. public opinion, and that as public support waned so did our leaders' resolve.

Direct or Indirect Approach? Where enemy vulnerabilities lead directly to his center of gravity we favor a direct approach; where his center of gravity is difficult to affect, we attack more available vulnerabilities as a way to ultimately expose that center of gravity.

Decisive Points. Sometimes geographic, sometimes points in time, correctly identifying and controlling decisive points gives us a major advantage. We gain momentum.

Culminating Points. The art of the attack is to secure the objective before reaching culmination—in layman's terms "running out of gas before the job is done." An attacker may reach culmination because of sheer physical exhaustion, the stiffening defense of the defender as large tracts of territory are lost, or the entry of other countries into the fray. In fact, the art of the defense is to draw in the attackers and strike when they have exhausted themselves or are ill disposed to defend. Both Napoleon and Hitler hit culminating points in their attacks on Russia—both with disastrous results. When weather and extended supply lines caused U.S. forces to temporarily culminate outside Bagdad in Gulf War II, the time was effectively used to rearm, refuel, rest, and then continue the battle.

Branches and Sequels. Strategists have to keep an eye on every possible development as the battle progresses. Some battles "branch" into new developments and every battle has a "sequel" or follow-on situation. Again using Gulf War II as an example, the strategists had to keep in mind questions like, "What if Saddam lobs Scuds into Israel? What will Iraq be like after the conflict?" We war-game all the possibilities in order to prepare for them.

Termination. Before forces are ever committed, leaders must visualize the end result and have a realistic expectation of achieving the desired outcome. Then they need an exit strategy. How do we know when the work is done? How do we get out of there? These are two very important questions.

Mission Analysis

Battle commanders visualize activities in time and space in the quest for the desired endstate. They translate that vision into missions and, through force of will, provide battlefield leadership that concentrates overwhelming combat power at the decisive time and place.

Battle commanders must be receptive to information, and have the cognitive and analytic skills to visualize endstates. They then formulate a concept of operations to guide and motivate their units to accomplish the mission. It's part art and part science. Properly analyzing the mission in the first place is a big part of our success.

Mission analysis is a beautiful thing, and the United States Military does it extremely well, primarily because we practice it so rigorously.

The technique is just what the name implies—taking a mission and analyzing the heck out of it to make sure we fully understand it. Understanding what we're being asked to do is that first important step to actually going out and doing it. It's ready, aim, fire, not the "ready, fire, aim" we often complain about.

You can apply this technique to your business, your body, or your life mission.

In the military we're normally responding to a mission passed to us from higher headquarters, as is often the case in business. Mission analysis also applies to the missions that derive from your personal vision—understanding your personal goals and objectives and what it will take to get them done.

Absolutely key to this process is fully understanding the issue of intent.

We want to understand the commander's intent two levels up. In other words, a colonel needs to understand what his two-star commander is thinking. What's the guy doing? What's he trying to accomplish? Where does my unit fit into the plan?

When a mission is received, we break it down into tasks. Some of the tasks are specified in a written order, so they're broken out and listed. But some of the tasks are implied, and have to be uncovered through careful analysis.

For instance, if the unit's mission is to take Hill 529, taking the hill is a specified task. But if the unit has to cross a river under fire to get to the hill, then crossing that river is an implied task—often a difficult one. When all the specified and implied tasks are listed, the truly essential tasks are determined and highlighted. The routine tasks are noted, but only the tasks that the unit must accomplish successfully in order to complete the mission are deemed essential.

Limitations and the degree of risk to be accepted are also considered. Limitations are restrictions that either must be done or cannot be done. Sometimes commanders will be told to "keep two companies in reserve," or "whatever you do, don't cross the highway." These restrictions limit the range of action and are important to understand. Similarly, commanders must understand how much risk they're being asked to accept, to both personnel and equipment. Will it be a fight-to-the-last-man mission or an economy of force where casualties must be kept to a minimum?

The commander, aided by staff, also takes an in-depth look at the area of operations—both by studying the map and by personal observation when possible. Terrain and weather are analyzed and enemy capabilities and vulnerabilities are mined for understanding. Facts and assumptions are identified and distinguished from one another. Obviously, assumptions are kept to the barest minimum and then scrutinized for validity and necessity. An assumption is valid only if it is deemed likely to occur, and it is considered necessary only if it is essential for the development of a plan. The temptation to assume away problems is insidious, and must be guarded against.

A thorough consideration of available assets is also part of the process. "What assets do I have to accomplish my mission?" is a common question. The commander and staff take careful inventory of the available assets and sometimes ask for more.

Of course, all analysis is done under the constraint of time, one of our most precious resources.

★ ★ ★   **STRATEGY 18**   ★ ★ ★

ANALYZE YOUR MISSION. Mission analysis is the art of breaking down your mission into tasks, and analyzing your assets and limitations. Understand the difference between a fact and an assumption. Know the risks involved. Mission analysis is hard, organized, realistic thinking about an endeavor. It leads to planning, and ultimately achievement.

Time Analysis

The leader must sometimes balance detailed planning against the speed and surprise of immediate action. Time analysis is an integral part of mission analysis and must be a continuous process, with techniques in place to maximize this expendable commodity.

Leaders need to know the amount of time available, both for the planning and execution phase of any mission. Time begins with the receipt of the mission and ends with mission accomplishment. The leader needs to know the unit's decision cycle—the amount of time it takes to analyze the mission, issue orders, and move out.

Deadlines help define the time parameter. When the staff has a time limit, they can allocate time accordingly.

One method for allocating time is reverse planning—reverse-listing tasks from the deadline to ensure there's time enough to get them all done. After allocating time for each task, the leader reorders the tasks from last to first, to make sure they all fit in the time available. There's no point structuring the front-end tasks, only to run out of time at the end. Reverse planning ensures there's time allocated for all the tasks—even when things are rushed.

Good commanders also give subordinate units time to plan. Their time must also be allocated; otherwise, believe me, the higher headquarters will hog all the planning time, leaving the executers little time to react.

We use what's known as the one-third–two-thirds rule. That is, each headquarters uses no more than one-third of the available planning time, leaving two-thirds of the time to subordinate units. When was the last time you saw that technique used? We're not as good as we should be, either. Hogging time is endemic to the human race.

Training units to plan on a timetable is the ultimate test of discipline. But the commander has a helper; it's called the "warning order."

Rather than waiting for their staff to complete mission analysis, commanders simply tell subordinate units what they know as soon as they know it. It may not be complete information, but it sure beats the heck out of not knowing anything.

"We're going to be moving out in a day or two," while tremendously incomplete, is infinitely better than ignorance. It at least gets a subordinate unit thinking and planning. Partial information is always better than no information.

Ultimately, the commander approves the results of mission analysis, deciding which tasks are essential, formulating a final mission statement, providing the focus for further planning, and finally—execution.

★ ★ ★ STRATEGY 19 ★ ★ ★

MAKE TIME MANAGEMENT A PRIORITY. Reverse-plan missions so you know how much time to allot to each task. Don't be a time hog—give others two-thirds of available planning time. Use "warning orders" to alert teammates to a new mission. Time is money; manage it as such.

Bringing It Home

The military method of breaking down missions can be applied to any number of life situations.

Let's take a tough one—the family move.

The Shermans, a family of four, have lived in the Midwest for ten years. Dad works for a pharmaceutical company and Mom teaches math at the local high school. Chad Sherman, 16, is a sophomore in high school, and his sister, Jennifer, is 14 and in eighth grade. Dad's being transferred to Atlanta.

The transfer isn't a total surprise, but it's still a big deal. The kids will leave their friends; Mom will have to find a new teaching job. Where to begin?

Fortunately, Mom and Dad have a common vision. In their mind's eye they see their new, house, neighborhood, church, and the high school their kids will attend. They see Mom's new school, too, and a short commute for Dad each day. The vision is based on their values, and the principles by which they live. High on the list of values is a quality high school experience for Chad and Jennifer.

Mom and Dad do a quick mission analysis. The first consideration is time. Is there enough time to do all that needs to be done before the kids' first day of school? For Mom to start her new teaching job? They do a quick time check and see that they have about six months to get everything done. Not a lot of time, but doable.

The tasks begin to pile up, both specified and implied. Send out résumés. Find real estate agent. Conduct garage sale. Sell house. Identify new neighborhoods. Buy a new house. Move household goods. They quickly reverse-order the tasks from the day the kids will start in their new high school. The essential tasks are identified: Sell house. Find Mom new job. Buy house. Move.

They look at a map of Atlanta. Finding Dad's new office, they explore outward in ever-expanding concentric circles, noting the highways and possible living areas. They're going to want a lot more information. Later, they'll do an Internet search, contact real estate agents, and talk to friends who've lived in Atlanta. Dad has a meeting there next month, so he'll have a chance to reconnoiter the area.

They consider their assets. Dad's company will pay for some of the move. The kids are old enough now to be a real help, as opposed to the last move when they were mostly in the way. The Shermans have two cars, and Chad recently got his driver's license. He could drive one of the family cars and Dad could drive a rental truck. They realize they want real estate agents at both ends.

The limitations on the mission are few. They have a rough idea of how much they can spend on a new house. They would like to limit their school search to public schools. They assume they can sell their current home for close to market value, but are willing to culminate the sales effort early if necessary by lowering their asking price.

They begin to see that the decisive points will occur with the sale of their house, the selection of a new house, the move itself, and acquiring Mom's new teaching job. Of these, they see the sale of their house as the center of gravity for the operation. Though much work will remain to be done, they see their children's first day at their new high school as the cap-stone event of the effort. Everything revolves around that event coming off as a positive experience.

It's time to give the kids a warning order.

Mom and Dad have conducted mission analysis, and they want to inform Chad and Jennifer immediately so that they, too, can begin planning.

The mission briefing goes well. Mom and Dad are surprised at their own enthusiasm for the mission, and the kids seem to recover quickly from their initial shock. They have lots of questions, which Mom and Dad field as best they can. "It's early, but we're going" is the basic theme.

Chad and Jennifer both come up with things that Mom and Dad hadn't thought of. More planning will be necessary, but now it's a team effort.

The desired endstate is clearer now; the mission is understood.

Your Tool Kit

There's a time and place for daydreaming, for brainstorming, for letting the creative juices flow. We need to cultivate environments that allow these important right-brain functions to impact the situation.

Probably, we need to do a better job in the U.S. Military with this. I always like to ask, "Is there a new, unconventional way we could do this mission and maybe save a lot of time and trouble?"

This isn't always necessarily popular with the same-old-way crowd, but it's important to challenge the conventional wisdom.

Human events are dynamic. The word *endstate* itself is a misnomer; we're always moving and growing.

The United States Military is in a business that tries to corral life, to make sense of its myriad challenges. We have to see the future, and impact it. It's a difficult job, so we're very focused on ways to structure it as best we can.

And now you know the mental tools of our trade.

Train Tough Challenge

Conduct a mission analysis of your next major undertaking. Consider specified and implied tasks, limitations, facts and assumptions, and your available assets. Reverse-plan your tasks, and allocate time accordingly.

6

—★—

LEARNING
No Such Thing as Graduation

I have studied the German all my life. I have read the memoirs of his generals and political leaders. I have even read his philosophers and listened to his music. I have studied in detail the accounts of every one of his damn battles. I know exactly how he will react under any given set of circumstances. He hasn't the slightest idea what I'm going to do. Therefore, when the day comes, I'm going to whip hell out of him.
—General George S. Patton

George Patton rightly receives credit as a blood-'n'-guts general, an inspirational leader of men and brilliant tactician. What few realize however, is the degree to which Patton dedicated himself to lifelong learning, to mastering the art and science of warfare.

George Patton stayed a student his entire career, and that's what you've got to do if you're serious about dominating your environment. Steep yourself in your career choice; develop an insatiable desire to know how the movers and shakers who came before you got it done. Follow their trail like a hound dog, sniffing out one prize after another, always on the hunt.

Don't get lazy. Don't sit on your degrees. Throw yourself into learning situations; suck up the nutrients. Find out who's building a better mousetrap and improve on their ideas.

Challenge yourself.

You never know what you don't know.

Think of that. Sometimes you really don't know what you don't know.

It's scary.

You can be cruising along feeling pretty good about yourself, but be missing key pieces of information, critical skills, even life-changing tech-niques—and not even know it!

The only way you're going to uncover these things is through learning, that messy, uncomfortable experience requiring time and energy. And guess what? There is no other way.

The only way to move forward is to learn.

And learning hurts. If it didn't hurt, everybody would be doing it.

Most people aren't interested in learning, or they learn at a very modest pace.

Because learning hurts.

Always has, always will.

We have to attack learning in the same way we attack any other goal, methodically and with a tremendous amount of energy.

The way George Patton did it.

The George S. Patton Learning System

Patton was motivated.

From an early age he saw himself as a warrior, a leader of men, a future general. At times this vision was so strong he felt as though he had been reincarnated from past lives on the battlefield. To say he had a strong sense of identity would be an understatement.

Patton didn't just pass through military schools, he swept through them like a tornado, sucking up energy and thought.

He built a personal library of military strategy and tactics. Alexander the Great. Frederick the Great. Ulysses S. Grant. Stonewall Jackson. Pat-ton studied them all. His books on Napoleon grew so multitudinous they came to be known as his "Napoleonic Collection."

Patton used margin notes and note cards to record his thoughts while reading, and he didn't always agree with what he read. "Bull!" was his most frequent entry, but he clearly studied with an eye toward how he himself would one day command—and he studied daily. "Always do your damnd-est," began one of his notebooks.

He enumerated the qualities of a good general. A general would be tac-tically aggressive and "love a good fight." He would demonstrate strength of character and steadiness of purpose. He would accept responsibility, exude energy, and maintain good health and strength.

Patton mastered strategy and tactics, and the mind-numbing nuances of military organization. He saw tanks as the dominant feature of future land warfare.

During World War I, Patton masterminded the U.S. tank school in France. He preached discipline, studied lessons learned from the French and British, and applied the lessons of history. He selected and trained officers, established unit organization and communications, and formulated the new strategy and tactics for mechanized warfare. It must have been some school. Patton later joined many of his own students in the world's first major tank battle, in 1917.

But Patton wasn't done learning.

He worked his way to Honor Graduate status at the Command and General Staff College, and his notes on the course became legendary. Two years later his pal Eisenhower had them in hand when he graduated at the top of his class. Both men were going places.

Patton was soon recognized as the most knowledgeable student of military history in the Army. His personal notes indicate he was even taking issue with Baron Carl von Clausewitz, the German master strategist, whose theories had dominated military thinking for a hundred years.

This wasn't one-dimensional learning.

Patton took what he learned and applied it to the world situation.

After training in Hawaii, Patton wrote a letter to the chief of staff at Fort Shafter, Hawaii, correctly detailing a Japanese attack, almost precisely as it would occur at Pearl Harbor—some four years later!

Patton became the master of German blitzkrieg tactics, studying everything about the new lightning warfare he could get his hands on and practicing the new mobile warfare in desert training. "Winners take risks!" was his strategic conclusion on the new warfare.

Once in battle, Patton demanded discipline from soldiers and a ferocious warrior spirit. He shared personal danger with his men and argued with Eisenhower for more risk taking. Promotions went to more steady generals, but Patton kept rolling up successes on the battlefield, making possible the early liberation of Paris and putting the Germans on the run.

Still, Patton kept learning, visiting ancient battle sites for inspiration and historical context. In Brittany he noted his route followed that of William the Conqueror, who had subdued rebellion in the area some 900 years before.

Patton corrected his own preconceived notions from early in the war, admitting the success of heavy artillery, telephone wire over radio, and the admission of female nurses into the combat zone.

By the time of the Battle of the Bulge, Patton's Third Army was fully engaged attacking Germans to the east. But Patton had learned an important lesson from his studies: Look beyond your assigned battle area for threats and opportunities. Patton kept an eye to the north, where he sensed the Germans were massing for a surprise attack. When all hell broke loose he already had a plan in place to counter the German advance.

No one thought it possible at the time, but Patton disengaged six of his divisions facing Germans to his front and swung them north into the flanks of the attacking Germans. They smashed the German offensive, arriving in time to rescue the Americans surrounded at Bastogne.

The German Army was never the same. Patton and his Third Army continued chasing them through Germany.

★★★ STRATEGY 20 ★★★

LEARN HOW TO LEARN. You learn what you want to learn. It's a question of desire, a sometimes uncomfortable process. It's not just sitting there—that's like getting stuck in a defensive mentality in the military. You've got to swing over to the offense and attack across a broad front—reading, listening, observing, performing. Attacking.

The United States Military Learning System

We learned a lot from George S. Patton. The U.S. Military committed itself to lifelong learning. Now we even have finishing schools for generals and sergeant majors. The G.I. Bill gives soldiers the opportunity to attend college throughout their military career and beyond.

The U.S. Military is no place for the young person who doesn't like to learn, because that's most of what we do. Of course, we do some very unique things to keep it interesting. We've learned that learning is more than knowledge. It's an experience that results in changed behavior and enhanced performance.

Patton became a lifelong learner because he loved what he was doing. From an early age he felt the call to battle. And that's an important point.

People learn what they want to learn. That's why, when we bring someone on board, we want to find out that person's interests and talents. With more than 200 military occupational specialties, we want a good fit. If you're bored with the fundamentals of your career choice, you're probably in the wrong business.

Our education system is based on doctrine, the way we fight. We want to fight the way we train, and train the way we fight. Doctrine provides the intellectual underpinning for the entire effort. A lot of our doctrine is based on what Patton proved on the battlefield—that once you engage the enemy, aggressive action carries the day. We want our three pillars of professional development—institutional learning, unit training, and self-study—to reflect that doctrine.

Institutional Learning

Military schools keep getting better.

At the start of my career there was too much rote learning. We were learning to do things better, but very often they were the wrong things.

We refocused on mission and doctrine, the American way of war.

Now the military learning environment is a more collaborative process, more focused on team. After basic training, our schools harness the experience of participants and become problem-centered. Instructors become team leaders. These more experienced individuals learn to capitalize on moments of truth, those "aha" moments where discovery learning takes place.

Importantly, our schools teach a common language, based on our doctrine. When we introduce a term like *battle space*, we want everyone in our military to know exactly what we mean. The profession of arms is exactly that—a profession. As in any profession, we have our own vocabulary. Our words mean things. And they need to mean the *same* thing to the Army, Navy, Air Force, and Marines. So we spend a lot of time and effort to teach our common language.

Military schools have a much different view of administration than in the typical American school district where teachers are squeezed between a domineering bureaucracy and the student-inmates running the asylum. Teachers see administration as a way up the success ladder, so they leave the classroom for the comforts of the office. Compare the administrator-to-student-to-teacher ratio in U.S. schools and you'll find that we lead the world in percentage of administrators.

In the military we believe the bureaucrats are there to serve us. Sure, we have administration, but it works *for* us, not the other way around. I spent some time as an administrator, and let me tell you, I was ridden hard and put away wet. We also keep the numbers of administrators down, so we always outnumber them. And we make sure their activities conform to the blood, sweat, and tears of the military mission and not the other way around.

Training in Units

The key to training in military units is making leaders trainers. Training is not something we farm out to a special department and say, "You figure it out." Leaders are the trainers.

Training is battle-focused. It's not a deal where someone says, "Gee, that might be fun. Let's do that."

No. Training is based on the unit's war plan, the tasks the unit performs when it goes to war.

Commanders take the war plan and determine the Mission Essential Task List (METL). The METL is comprised of the seven or eight tasks that a unit must be able to perform in battle. An engineer battalion, for instance, might have "support river crossing operations," as one of its METL tasks.

Commanders assess how well their units can perform the METL tasks, grading each task as "Trained," "Untrained," or "Partially Trained."

From the METL assessment, a commander crafts his training strategy. In his mind he sees his unit excelling on the battlefield. That's the vision. Then he asks the question, "How do we get there?"

The answer is the training strategy. Good commanders want training to be challenging; that's the only way their unit will improve. They want training to be performance-oriented, not multiple choice. The key is to train as you fight—in accordance with the doctrine. Commanders enforce standards but allow honest mistakes.

They centralize planning to keep the unit focused on the wartime mission, but decentralize execution to allow subordinate leaders to focus on their particular strengths and weaknesses.

They ensure external resources and support are available to their unit and ruthlessly protect the unit from training distracters. They are personally involved in training. It's their number one priority.

Good commanders have a plan. Both long- and short-range. They review the METL assessment and take a "crawl, walk, run" approach to the tasks. Some training will be basic, some will be refresher, and some will be sustainment training. But the battle focus will always be there.

Good commanders stress fundamentals. Can the unit *move, shoot,* and *communicate?* Can it *sustain* and *protect* itself?

They stress individual skills *and* teamwork.

One of the key links between the individual and the unit team is the *battle drill.*

We learned a lot about battle drills from the former Soviet Union.

The Soviets weren't the most creative force on the battlefield, but they were relentless. They wanted their military to follow a central command structure and to plow forward at all costs. They trained their army to function under stress, without rest, and without a whole lot of thought. They perfected the art of the battle drill—the ability to perform instantaneously, on instinct. They drilled and drilled and drilled.

The more we observed them, the more we saw the logic of what they were doing.

Combat is draining and disorienting. Some things you just have to be able to do by rote.

Respond to enemy air attack is a sample battle drill. The unit repeatedly drills their response until an enemy air attack is just another day at the mill. It becomes a battle drill.

Finally, the commander assesses training performance. Sometimes assessment comes in the form of a critique, where the unit is measured against definitive standards. But it rarely becomes a lecture on what went wrong.

Commanders use After Action Reviews (AARs) as a structured review process so that participants discover for themselves what happened, why it happened, and how it can be done better. AARs are guided discussions focused on the training objectives. Unit members describe what happened in their own words and from their own point of view. Alternative courses of action that might have been more effective are introduced. The intent is not to embarrass or humiliate, but to allow everyone to learn from both success and mistakes—and to gain an appreciation for some of the challenges of leadership.

By the end of the AAR, everyone understands what was good, bad, and average about the training. The art of the AAR process is to get participants to accurately assess their own performance. We've found there's nothing like self-assessment to get warriors motivated to improve. The leaders reinforce the lessons learned with an eye to the unit's confidence and cohesion—and they plan future training to sustain and improve performance.

Self-Development

This is where Patton excelled. He didn't spend any more time in military schools than his contemporaries, but he made the most of it. Then he used self-directed study to optimize his unit training and, just as important, to prepare himself for the rigors of generalship.

He was always reading, studying the nuances of military strategy and tactics.

You need to be reading too. It's one of the most productive activities I know. Reading is amazing.

Think of it this way: How better to get into someone else's mind or experience than to read your way in?

Do I want to actually live Robert Eichelberger's experience at Buna? Or Patton's at the Bulge?

Not really.

But I sure want to read about it. I want to know what it was like, what they thought, and how they reacted. But I want to do it without the mosquitos or the snow.

So I read.

How better to get inside the head of Eichelberger, Patton, Washington, Napoleon, Grant, Eisenhower, MacArthur, or any number of great leaders, innovators, or scoundrels?

Other than the occasional documentary, nothing compares with reading.

Having a personal library is a tremendous asset. So is access to a public library. No doubt your taxes are paying for one. Might as well get your money's worth.

I take the books I read and reduce them to the back of a 3 by 5 card. I want to remember what I read. Some books warrant a whole slew of cards. I'm up to a couple feet's worth. Once a year I study the whole collection. If I know I'm going to be stuck someplace, I pull out an inch of cards and spend the time reviewing. I consider the books I've read to be an integral part of who I am. They represent the places I've visited and the minds I've explored. Eventually I'll load the entire collection onto my PDA.

Of course not everybody learns in the same way. Reading is just one way, albeit an important one. There's also listening, observing, and performing.

And the much overlooked process of mentorship.

Mentoring a Tiger

Lieutenant Colonel Earl Woods retired from the United States Army in 1974. He served two tours in Vietnam, the second as a Green Beret. He taught military history to ROTC cadets at City College New York. Throughout his career, Earl Woods always wanted his soldiers to know what they were doing—and why.

Colonel Woods often expresses pride in his military experience, the fact that he made a commitment and kept it. He learned discipline and the value of teamwork.

As a forty-two-year-old lieutenant colonel, he took up golf.

A few years later, a son was born to Earl and Tida Woods. They named him Tiger, after a South Vietnamese lieutenant colonel with whom Earl had grown close in Vietnam.

From the very beginning, golf became a way for Earl and Tiger to spend time together.

But then Earl saw the talent—Tiger was a natural.

The swing came easily. The hand-eye coordination was exceptional. And the confidence! From the start young Tiger loved to compete, and to learn. His level of desire was remarkable.

Earl Woods developed a strategy. Drawing on the full range of his military experience, he developed the most nurturing environment possible to assist young Tiger.

First came sacrifice. Earl and Tida put Tiger's needs ahead of their own.

Earl became Tiger's practice companion and teacher, a function he learned to love teaching cadets. He was careful to let the impetus for learning come from Tiger, as opposed to pushing, the trap into which parents so often fall.

He taught Tiger about the clubs in the bag using military reverse planning. Since most strokes are saved with the short game, Earl reasoned that it made sense to start there. He wanted Tiger to see each golf hole from green to tee rather than from tee to green. That way, he was setting up putts as opposed to just seeing how far he could hit the ball. Tiger learned to reverse plan each hole.

The preshot routine became standard operating procedure (SOP in military jargon). In the U.S. Military, we study a procedure, refine it, and perfect it until it becomes SOP. Earl did the same thing with Tiger's setup and swing.

And there was no free swinging. Like the marksman he had been in the Army, Earl emphasized the importance of having a target, and developing the discipline and technique to hit that target.

Finally, Green Beret that he was, Earl developed a course in mental toughness. With Tiger's agreement, he used every trick in the book to distract Tiger's play. Golf is a game of concentration, and often the slightest distraction can upset a player's focus. Tiger experienced the full gamut, learning to perform under the most trying circumstances. Mental toughness. Discipline. These were things a Green Beret could teach like no other.

To his credit, Earl Woods also understood his own limitations in teaching the game of golf. He made sure Tiger got proper instruction in the golf nuances that only a teaching professional can provide.

As Tiger matured into a golfing sensation, Earl found himself vetting Tiger's schedule with its myriad media demands. In this he was well prepared too, for Earl Woods was a graduate of the Department of Defense Information School, a course that trains officers to work with media.

Tiger Woods is one in a million, maybe one in a billion. He clearly has a physical gift, a powerful love for the game of golf, and an intense desire to compete—and win. Tiger Woods is the product of numerous factors, no one of which explains his incredible rise to the top of his profession. But he has clearly benefited from the Earl Woods School of Golf, a program based on tried and tested military principles and a military mind-set.

And one more thing.

It's impossible to look at Tiger and Earl's relationship without seeing positive, consistent character development. At each step in the journey, Earl shared his value system. From the Tiger Woods Foundation to the way Tiger conducts himself on the course, it's clear that Earl's example has had an impact. Duty. Honor. Respect. Integrity. Personal courage.

Like father, like son.

★ ★ ★ **STRATEGY 21** ★ ★ ★

GET INTO SELF-DEVELOPMENT. Read. Study. Review. Improve. George S. Patton did. Open your own "Center for Lessons Learned" so you develop a mentality of constant learning. You won't know what you don't know until you ask the right questions. Developing your mind is the key to enhancing performance.

The Center for Lessons Learned

There are two kinds of nations: those who learn from war and those who do not. Those who face the myriad unpleasantries of reality, and those who stick their head in the sand.

What worked? What didn't work? Why?

These are the questions the services ask at their respective Centers for Lessons Learned. It's not critiquing; it's not assigning blame. We just want to know what happened, how to reinforce what worked, and how to fix what didn't.

We send out monitoring teams for each operation to collect firsthand information. We want them right where the action is, not listening to the brass spin something after it's already happened.

We looked at every phase of Gulf War II—from the force buildup to deployment to combat, all the way to stability operations. We apply a rigorous thought process to all the information gathered. That's how we learn.

We know our Army attack helicopters had problems in Iraq. They got shot up, and some of them got shot down and the crews captured. That didn't tend to happen with the Air Force's fixed-wing aircraft. Maybe attack helicopters are going to continue to have problems when they're shot at. We'll either have to modify them, or use them in a different manner.

Special forces proved their value, identifying bombing targets and effectively finding the path of least resistance into Baghdad. We learned some time ago the necessity of putting people on the ground instead of relying only on satellite information. Now that lesson learned is paying off.

Our communications worked superbly, a far cry from the problems we had in the 1983 Grenada operation, when the services couldn't even talk to each other. Problem solved. We also did a great job disrupting Iraqi communications, a great improvement from Gulf War I.

The smart bombs worked, and laser-guided munitions reduced friendly fire casualties. But we need more air refueling capability. These are just a few of the big-picture lessons learned.

We also examine the tactics, techniques, and procedures to see what worked and what didn't. Sometimes we garner new insights, and sometimes we confirm what we learned in previous efforts. What we find impacts the future and the way we do business.

At rock bottom, we're on a search for the truth. By having our teams out there in the field we have a chance to see and experience what's happening. We can get to the truth and adjust fire accordingly.

Make sure you've got the same mentality for your business, your body, and your life.

Get to the truth. Act on it. Make learning a way of thinking and a way of life.

It works.

Train Tough Challenge

Start a self-development program.

★ Go to the library. Get a library card. Check out some books.

★ Reduce the books to a 3 by 5 card. That is, find the important thoughts in a book and keep them on your cards.

Commit to lifelong learning. You never know what you don't know!

7

———★———

PROBLEM SOLVING

We're Here to Fix Things!

When directed to do a thing, if you can't do it at first, do not at once report you can't do it, but try some other way, and keep on trying some other way until you have either succeeded or have exhausted every possible means you can think of. It is really astonishing how comparatively few things in this world cannot be done, if one really wants to do them and tries hard enough to do them.
    —Noncommissioned Officers Manual, 1917

We really are here to fix things. It's in our human being job description: "Breaks things. Fixes things. Fixes things other people break. Sometimes fixes things that ain't broke."

If you're not solving problems, making decisions, and fixing things, you're dead. Problems are part of the human landscape. We can't wish them away, and, if we could, we'd be bored stiff, though it's hard to tell that to someone with a flat tire.

The history of mankind can be traced through our ever-increasing capacity to create—and solve—problems. The tools get better; the mind struggles to keep up.

Problems create emotion. We grow tired of problems because they're emotionally draining. We wish they'd all just go away.

But they won't.

One of the most challenging things about life in the military is the amazing number of problems we confront, their dazzling variety, and the often terrible conditions in which we confront them. It's sometimes all we can do to keep it from becoming a complicated mess.

We work very hard to keep our emotions in check, to react cooly in tough situations. We've developed problem-solving and decision-making processes that keep us centered. We speak a common language and practice team response techniques, so when push comes to shove we can push and shove right back.

Over time, we've learned there's an art and science to problem solving. The art is the creative right-brain function that discovers unique solutions to new situations; the science is the plodding left-brain function that organizes, and methodically works a problem to resolution. We need the best of both worlds.

We've found some innovative ways to slice and dice problems. But what we find at the bottom of every problem solved is always the same—human motivation. How bad does the guy with the flashlight want to go down in the hole to fix the problem? The answer tells you a lot about how things will go. Ultimately, you gotta want it.

Swede Momsen, U.S. Navy Problem Solver

Charles "Swede" Momsen graduated from the U.S. Naval Academy in 1919 and joined the submarine corps at a time when submariners were the second-class citizens of the Navy. He grew tired of explaining that neither he nor any of his ancestors were from Sweden, yet with his blond hair and fair complexion the moniker "Swede" stuck to him like flypaper. Once the Navy gives you a nickname, it's yours for life.

But that was the least of the problems the Navy would present to Swede Momsen.

From the beginning of his career as a submariner, Momsen was plagued by a simple question: "If a submarine sinks and can't resurface, how do we get out?"

Given the technology of the time, the Navy didn't have much of an answer. It was considered bad form to ask the question at all, akin to what we call *whining* today.

Swede was in command of a nearby sub when the *S-51* sank in 1925 with all hands aboard. There was nothing to be done about the trapped submariners, but it made a life-changing impression on Swede.

In the ten-year period leading up to World War II, the Navy lost 700 crew members in twenty submarine accidents. Submarine duty became known as the "Coffin Service."

Swede Momsen went to work on the problem, designing a rescue bell that could be lowered by cable to a crippled sub, and secured by bolts to an escape hatch. He diagramed the concept and sent it up the chain of command—where it was summarily disapproved.

In 1927 another sub, the *S-4*, sank in 110 feet of water. The men were heard tapping for three days before they too fell silent. Swede was part of the investigation team that eventually raised the sub, and he was tasked to answer letters from the crew's family members.

The incident spurred interest in submarine rescue, and Momsen soon found service with the Navy's Submarine Safety Test Unit. At the time, the Navy saw submarine rescue as something that happened from above, perhaps by raising a crippled sub. Momsen took a different approach to the problem.

What if sailors escaped from below? How would they breathe? Could they survive the bends?

The answer was Momsen's Submarine Escape Lung, which came to be known simply as the "Momsen Lung." The small rubber bag contained a canister of soda lime to remove poisonous carbon dioxide and replenish the air with oxygen. The contraption hung around a sailor's neck, strapped at the waist. It not only provided air to breathe, but its buoyancy carried a submariner slowly to the surface, thus preventing the bends.

Swede led the way in testing his new device, often at great personal risk. He simulated ascents from as far as 300 feet below the surface, and then took to the Potomac River for more trials. In the process he devised a bell for submerging, and began to see this new device as another possible rescue apparatus.

Momsen's work was drawing national media coverage by that point, and the Navy approved more tests. But the question of how a submariner might actually exit a submarine had yet to be addressed.

The *S-4*, formerly a deathtrap for submariners, was pressed back into service. A hatch was installed in the motor room with the idea of flooding the compartment through valves until compressed air opened the hatch. In theory, enough air would remain at the top of the compartment to allow the men to breathe prior to their escape.

Momsen and his crew of divers tested the system off the Florida Keys, at one point effecting an escape from 207 feet. The Navy was soon constructing escape hatches for every submarine in the inventory.

Swede continued working on his rescue bell, reminding his Navy superiors that he had presented the idea years before. He received the go-ahead and soon had a prototype in hand. The idea was to lower the bell with two cables, accompanied by a diver who would guide it to the sub. There, a steel collar and rubber gasket would seal the bell to the escape hatch. Small groups of crew members could then be carried to the surface—and safety.

After dangerous testing, Momsen's bell was perfected. The Navy ordered one built for every fleet in the Navy. Perhaps as a snub to Swede's antibureaucratic modus operandi and the notoriety he received for the Momsen Lung, the Navy dubbed his bell the McCann Rescue Chamber.

Still, when the going got tough, the Navy called on Swede Momsen.

In May 1939 the submarine *Squalus* sank five minutes into a dive off the coast of New Hampshire, in 243 feet of water. The twenty-six men in the aft of the sub were drowned, but thirty-three survivors huddled in the forward section awaiting their fate.

Momsen was assigned to the Washington Navy Yard at the time, conducting underwater experiments with a team of divers. He was flown to the scene to direct the diving portion of the rescue attempt. The USS *Falcon* arrived with a team of divers and a rescue bell. In icy cold water and heavy seas, the stage was set for one of the most dramatic problem-solving events in naval history.

And there would be plenty of problems.

An admiral wanted to send a doctor down with the bell. Swede talked him out of it. Food, blankets, and carbon dioxide absorbent were more important, he reasoned, with one less life at risk.

It would take five trips to bring up the survivors, but with the worsening weather Momsen decided to try it in four. At the end of the last dive the cable was reduced to a single strand, but Momsen's superb guidance on ballast and buoyancy saved the day—and the final eight men rose to the surface.

Swede was then put in charge of salvaging the *Squalus*, a Herculean task, requiring the supervision of fifty-eight divers in 640 dives. The *Squalus* was more than one hundred meters long, half full of water, and embedded twenty feet into the ocean floor. There were fifteen miles of open sea between the sub and the nearest port, and it would have to be towed through treacherous shoals. The operation took months, but Swede and his team got the job done—without a death or serious injury. The *Squalus* was refitted and saw service in World War II as the USS *Sailfish*.

On the morning of December 7, 1941, Swede Momsen was one of the first to be awakened at Pearl Harbor. He survived the attacks and was charged with helping organize the new Pacific command that would respond to the war with Japan.

He then returned to submarine duty.

When it was discovered that U.S. torpedoes were not detonating on their targets, Momsen took the bull by the horns. He fired torpedoes into the cliffs of a Hawaiian island, personally retrieved a dud, and at great personal risk took apart the triggering device to discover the problem.

Design flaw. The firing pins weren't striking the primer cap with enough force.

Rather than wait for the industrial bureaucracy to correct the situation, Swede had the firing pins shortened in the machine shops at Pearl Harbor. Problem solved.

In the fall of 1943 Swede Momsen tested a new system of submarine warfare against Japanese shipping. Consisting of three-sub team warfare, his "wolf pack" technique was a resounding success. Swede was awarded the Navy Cross and summoned to Washington for a special assignment—fix the Navy mail system.

The mail mission was a disappointment, as Swede had been expecting a high command. But the mail problem had become political and was impacting sailor morale. Swede revamped the Navy's mail system in 90 days. He was soon back at sea, this time captaining the flagship of the Pacific Fleet.

Swede continued solving problems.

Freak explosions had badgered the Navy throughout the war. Swede reasoned that it might be static electricity created by silk bags of gunpowder touching the steel drums in which they were packed. Tests proved him correct. Once again his technical acumen, ability to visualize problems in their simplest form, and dogged determination were rewarded.

After the war, all of Swede Momsen's learned problem-solving acumen came to fruition in a radically new submarine concept. He even got the politics right.

In a Navy still dominated by a surface-ship mentality, Swede knew better than to try a frontal assault. So he tried the indirect approach.

He designed a sub that the surface ships could train against. It was faster, more agile, and could stay down longer.

It became the prototype for the modern nuclear sub that we know today.

Swede Momsen died in 1967 having known more than his share of problems. What made him unique was his uncanny ability to solve them.

The man was a problem-solving machine.

Next time you're in a pickle, you might try asking yourself, "*What would Swede Momsen do in a situation like this?*"

★ ★ ★   **STRATEGY 22**   ★ ★ ★

BECOME A PROBLEM SOLVER. Problem solving is part art and part science, fueled by desire. Make sure your emotions are spurring you to action and not getting in the way. When you sense emotional dissonance, take a moment and think. See if you can rearrange things so you're accessing emotions as fuel and not putting out emotional wildfires. Ask yourself, "What would Swede Momsen do in a situation like this?"

The United States Army Problem-Solving School

The year was 1827, and Henry Leavenworth had a problem.

His orders told him to establish a permanent cantonment on the left bank of the Missouri River—in Missouri. But the more he snooped around, the less inviting the east side of the river looked. It was low-lying land, swampy, and full of mosquitoes.

So Henry Leavenworth did what U.S. Army officers are always encouraged to do in uncertain situations: He applied common sense and initiative and followed the spirit of his orders, rather than the letter. He erected his cantonment on the west side of the river, on high ground, in Kansas.

Fort Leavenworth has been in Kansas ever since, grappling with the same kind of problems that confronted Colonel Leavenworth more than 175 years ago.

Most of the great military leaders in American history have been schooled there—Patton, Eisenhower, MacArthur, Eichelberger, and Colin Powell, to name a few.

The year-long Command and General Staff College is a wicket through which every Army major must pass en route to lieutenant colonel. Select Navy, Air Force, and Marine officers also attend the course, as do about one hundred allied officers. Everyone wants a piece of the American way of war, because nobody makes it like we do.

Battle staffs come to train at the National Simulation Center, applying decision-making and problem-solving processes in simulated war games against a hostile, thinking enemy. The Center for Army Lessons Learned is there, and so is the Combined Arms Research Library. At first blush a library might not seem terribly important to the Army, until you consider the vast history of past battles that it holds. And Army officers do a lot of reading . . . and study.

There are a number of high-speed schools at Fort Leavenworth, but the darling of the past two decades is the Combined Arms and Services Staff School (CAS3). I was an instructor there for three glorious years, helping turn young officers into problem solvers. Every captain in the Army goes to CAS3. For most, it's an excruciating process. In the space of five weeks CAS3 hits them with more problems than most people see in a year.

There are group problems and individual problems, military problems and nonmilitary problems. Problems that are well defined, solvable by calculations, and problems that are ill defined, requiring a more sophisticated skill set.

The staff groups consist of twelve captains and a lieutenant colonel, who guides them through the proceedings. Good staff groups soon learn the value of teamwork and leadership. Leader positions are rotated to keep everyone on their toes. Communication skills are also key, not only among staff members but in presenting recommendations and solutions to the colonel. Some products are presented in writing, others in an oral briefing. Form and content go hand in hand.

The captains learn research techniques and how to critically analyze information. They grapple with the latest military doctrine, procedures, and techniques. They're also encouraged to throw out inhibitions and brainstorm. Many times the best solution is not apparent at first blush. They have to open up and get beyond their usual blind spots, blockages, and prejudices. They learn to change perspectives and look at things in a different way. Open minds are fertile minds.

The captains master a variety of problem-solving techniques. They discover the importance of staying visually centered on all the facts and nuances of a particular effort. Visual centering encourages them to use chalkboards, bulletin boards, and other visual aids to keep them focused on the process.

Information is posted where it can be seen and shared by all, freeing group members to interact with the information rather than strain to remember it. They learn to guard against groupthink, that soothing, affirming process where everyone agrees—and everyone is dead wrong. Dissenting opinions must be welcomed and embraced or disposed of as the situation warrants.

Good staff groups learn time management. They budget their time, reverse plan, and assign a timekeeper to advise them on their progress. They're the groups who make time for lunch, a workout, and a movie— while others spiral into overtime. Procrastinators don't have a chance.

The beauty of the CAS3 problem-solving process is that it arranges problems in a way that makes them manageable. Solutions make more sense, are more easily communicated, and are more effectively defended.

Gut decisions still have their place, but that place is more defined. There are times when group decisions are more appropriate, such as when participants are equals; times when leaders must make decisions on the advice of staff; and decisions that are individual and personal.

The experience level of the decision maker is important too. We would trust the judgment of a seasoned major over that of a green lieutenant. But in either case we want to structure problems in a way that optimizes the application of our intelligence, values, and gut feelings.

The CAS3 Problem-Solving Process

Let's take a look at the CAS3 problem-solving process. We'll keep it Bender simple.

Define the Problem. Which problem are you solving? Is it *whether* to purchase a new battle tank—or *which* new battle tank to buy? These are two very different questions. It's usually better to struggle with problem definition at the beginning, in a brainstorm mode, than to have to start over after you've done a lot of work. The problem statement addresses the "who, what, when, where" of the issue and is stated in the infinitive. Something like, "To determine the best main battle tank for Fort Knox to purchase during 2004 to replace our aging fleet."

Gather Information. It's time to research. Time to test the captain's creativity in finding and presenting germane information. From the Internet to the interview, our captain begins his quest for truth. He'll break his information into facts and assumptions. Obviously facts are safer than assumptions. Facts must stand alone and be relevant to the problem. Assumptions are conditions he can't verify. He has to be careful not to assume away the problem. Here are some examples:

> **Fact.** Higher headquarters says we can't get more money.

> **Assumption.** We can't get more money.

Develop Courses of Action. This step can be relatively simple, as in the case of listing main battle tank options. It can also be incredibly complex, as in developing courses of action for accomplishing a mission on the battlefield. In the latter case the challenge is to generate courses of action that are workable, and significantly different from each other.

Develop Criteria. The criteria are based on our facts and assumptions, and come in two types—screening and evaluation criteria.

> **Screening criteria** are the absolute standards that the courses of action must pass to solve the problem. In the case of the main battle tank, we might have an absolute limit on cost and be limited by the Buy American Act. So we might find ourselves screening out tanks that cost over our budget that are not American made.

> **Evaluation criteria** are used to measure and evaluate the remaining courses of action. Cost might continue to be an evaluation criterion in our main battle tank decision, as saving money would most certainly continue as a consideration. Firepower, dependability, and maneuverability are examples of other evaluation criteria we might use. We'll rank-order and then weight the criteria so we know each criterion's relative importance. We'll use benchmarks to determine the point at which a course of action becomes an advantage.

Analyze and Compare Courses of Action. We analyze each course of action using the evaluation criteria. The advantages and disadvantages of each course of action are considered and listed. Then we compare the courses of action. Various software programs are available to help us weight the criteria and quantify the comparison, but many times our choice is apparent by this point.

Choose the Best Course of Action. Following the problem-solving process provides a depth of knowledge and confidence the captain wouldn't otherwise possess. He can now make his choice—and defend his decision—based on the analysis.

One of the beauties of the CAS3 process is that it lends itself so well to oral and written communication: oral in the form of a decision briefing, written in the form of a staff study. While there's always the danger of groupthink, we at least have an approach to problem solving that everybody in the Army understands—as well as common formats for communicating recommendations. It's a giant step forward from swagging it.

★ ★ ★   **STRATEGY 23**   ★ ★ ★

DEFINE PROBLEMS. The U.S. Military favors a methodical approach to problem solving, but we leave room for creativity. Brainstorm. Use visual centering to stay focused. Develop techniques for drawing out the thoughts and ideas of others. Watch out for groupthink. When working with a team, make sure you've got a solid definition of the problem you're trying to solve. It will help in your time management.

We're Here to Fix Things!

Problem solving, decision-making, and just plain fixing things are not always reducible to a formula. Life moves much too fast for that.

That's why the Swede Momsen story is so endearing.

Swede got to the bottom of things because he cared. He saw his buddies trapped, with no hope, and decided to do something about it. He witnessed dud torpedoes and got into the water, fished one out, took it apart—and fixed it.

As he grappled with bureaucracy his political skills improved. He developed into a master strategist and tactician. He had the motivation to learn what it took to succeed, to solve problems, and to advance the cause of freedom.

Swede had his share of setbacks, but as a problem solver he's tough to beat.

Train Tough Challenge

1. Use the CAS3 Problem-Solving Process on your next complex problem.

2. Next time you're stumped on a problem, ask yourself, "What would Swede Momsen do in a situation like this?"

8

———— ★ ————

ETHICS

One Dilemma After Another

Integrity is the most important responsibility of command. Commanders are dependent on the integrity of those reporting to them in every decision they make. Integrity cannot be ordered but it can be achieved only by encouragement and example.
General John D. Ryan, U.S. Air Force

On the face of it, the U.S. Military would be the last place you would go for moral instruction. We deal in death and destruction and the implements thereof. The average American can point to several instances where we lost our way. Besides, ethics is boring.

So let's get real.

Let's exclude the less than 1 percent of Americans who are pacifists, who see all things military as inherently evil. I respect their right to their opinion, even though I find it socially irresponsible. To my mind they're living in a make-believe world, leaving the rest of us to grapple with the tough issues. They're not reading this book anyway.

The world is, always has been, and probably will remain a very dangerous place. Idiots abound, and there's never any shortage of other idiots to follow them. At some point, in some fashion, nations need a military, just as every burgh and hamlet has a police force. Sorry about that, but that's the way it is. Maybe someday it will change, but I'm not holding my breath.

Given that we have to have a military, the next question is, when should we go to war? What is a just war? What is an unjust war?

OK. That was three questions.

And I'm not going to try and answer any of them, even though they're central questions for our government and the American people. The answers define who we are and what's important to us, and yes, we discuss these questions in the military.

But they're not as instructive as the central question that the U.S. Military contends with in every moment of our existence. And that question is this: Given that we have the mission of defending the United States of America, and that we are entrusted with tremendous destructive power in carrying out that mission, how ought we to do business?

How ought we to do business?

That's the question.

And the answers are anything but boring.

The Truth as a Way of Life

After the Vietnam debacle the U.S. Military painstakingly rededicated itself to the truth. It hurt. I know. I was there for the adjustment period.

Vietnam was America's nightmare. Twelve excruciating years of indecisive war, based on bad information and lies.

I don't disparage the sacrifices of our soldiers or the intentions of our leaders. In fact I honor both. We tried.

But clearly we lost our way.

We started lying, first to ourselves and then to others. We lied in the White House, in the Pentagon, and then in the field. The more we lied, the tougher it became to confront the truth. And we were paying for the lies in human lives. Enemy body counts were inflated; the credibility gap was created.

It was a depressing time. Go back and watch the movies of the period; few of them had happy endings. The moral relativism of the 1960s came to full bloom in the Vietnam experience. The military reflected the society of the time—riddled with drugs and other means of escape. We were watching the same stuff on TV and in the movies, and listening to the same music. Most of the movies made about the war play the music of the time in the background. It was pervasive, influential, and often ironic.

There were many low points, but the gruesome details of the My Lai massacre were unparalleled. How could American troops be reduced to killing unarmed women and children? How could the cover-up have been so thoroughly orchestrated throughout the chain of command?

Clearly, something was wrong.

As the smoke cleared and the leadership changed, we set about looking for answers.

What we found was that over the long years of ambiguous battle we had succumbed, at every level, to expediency. We lost respect for the truth.

And the only way out was to get back to that truth. It was a hard road.

To fix the credibility gap we embarked on a "glad you asked" campaign. This was something deeply countercultural to the mentality of the time, and it was tough to implement. It was a philosophy of openness, that welcomed questions from the media and others, that ultimately gave us a fresh start with the truth.

We also returned to American history, not only to review our battlefield successes but to rediscover our values. Loyalty. Duty. Respect. Selfless service. Honor. Integrity. Personal courage. They're all part of the plus side of our history.

These were the values we wanted to define our military, to be our compass for character development and ethical reasoning. We needed to trust each other with these values and to have them form the basis for building trust with the American people.

We knew we couldn't just preach these values, we had to demonstrate them. The values had to be something the troops could see and feel from the leadership, meaning leadership by example.

Values training had to take place across the board, at every level of the hierarchy. Even though the values are the same for privates and the generals, the challenges and responsibilities are different. Privates and generals also learn differently and have different starting points. The idea was to work ethics training into everything we do, from basic training to the war colleges. It had to become a way of life.

Basic Training in Values

The first day for soldiers in the Army begins at a reception battalion. There they learn about soldiering and military life: living in barracks, eating in a dining facility, and doing things the Army way. Army values are introduced at orientation, and we issue our recruits the Army Core Values Card—a personal frame of reference they can carry in their wallets.

The stay at the Reception Station is brief, but important. Nine weeks of basic training immediately follows. The soldiers are introduced to their drill sergeant, a living, breathing example of what they, too, can become. That drill sergeant will help train their minds and bodies to peak levels, instilling U.S. Military values each step of the way. It's a grueling nine weeks, with values training embedded at every turn.

Week One: The Values. The soldiers take their first physical fitness test, prepare their barracks for inspection, learn to march, and are taught how to disassemble, assemble, clean, and sight the M-16A2 rifle. They learn about special and general orders and the Military Justice System that now governs their behavior. As they adjust to military life, they are also taught the importance of our *value system* and how the system will shape them as soldiers.

Week Two: Loyalty. The soldiers learn unarmed combat skills, first aid, map reading, and land navigation. Their confidence is tested at Victory Tower—where they rappel from a thirty-foot platform. They learn *loyalty*—dedication to carry out unit missions and to serve the values of the United States, the Army, and the unit. Loyalty is presented as the precondition for trust, teamwork, and comradeship.

Week Three: Duty. Bayonet training. Marksmanship. Physical training and defensive actions against chemical attack are emphasized. Historical examples teach the importance of *duty*—accomplishing all tasks to the fullest of one's ability. Importantly, soldiers are also taught that they not only have the right to disobey illegal or immoral orders, they have a duty to do so. Nothing we teach them or order them to do relieves them of the responsibility to think—and make moral judgments.

Week Four: Respect. Physical strength is put to the test in a second physical fitness test, demonstrating progress from week one. Basic marksmanship fundamentals are practiced in detail, as is multiple-target selection. *Respect* is emphasized—the promotion of dignity, consideration of others, fairness, and equal opportunity. Soldiers are admonished never to take advantage of authority when placed in charge of others.

Week Five: Selfless Service. M-16A2 rifle qualification. Soldiers qualify as Marksman, Sharpshooter, or Expert. They learn the value of *selfless service* and how other soldiers have given of themselves throughout U.S. history. They're reminded that the welfare of the nation and mission accomplishment come before personal safety or comfort. Selfless service does not preclude a healthy ego or a sense of ambition. It does, however, preclude selfish careerism.

Week Six: Honor. Soldiers experience a variety of sophisticated weapons, learn tactics, and participate in a defensive live-fire exercise. They also learn the meaning of *honor*—the will to make moral decisions based on deep personal values and conscience. Honor is a state of being possessed by those upholding the values of a moral code.

Week Seven: Integrity. Soldiers take their final physical fitness test and overcome the obstacles of the Confidence Course. They also learn the importance of *integrity*—honesty in word and deed, as well as being frank, open, and sincere with peers, subordinates, and seniors. Integrity fosters trust, authenticity, and the meeting of commitments. It means avoiding wrong and standing up for what is right.

Week Eight: Personal Courage. Soldiering skills are tested during the Warrior Field Training Exercise. Competence and confidence are demonstrated in each task—as is *personal courage,* the manifestation of physical and moral bravery. Fear must be controlled in both physical and moral contexts, and responsibility must be accepted for decisions, actions, mistakes, and shortcomings. Problems must be confronted directly and ethically, often when others counsel the easy way out.

Week Nine: Celebrating the Values. Soldiers should feel empowered by their training, ready to contribute to the team. They prepare for graduation

---

★ ★ ★   **STRATEGY 24**   ★ ★ ★

WEAVE ETHICAL CONSIDERATIONS INTO EVERYTHING. It's a way of thinking and a way of life. It's a search for truth and an openness to examination. Establish what your values are. They may not be Army values, but the Army list is a great place to start. Loyalty. Duty. Respect. Selfless service. Honor. Integrity. Personal courage.

---

with a sense of purpose. On graduation day they share a sense of pride different from any they have had before. They know now that the American people demand a high-quality military that honors the values of the Constitution and that respects the rule of law, human dignity, and individual rights. They are sworn to the highest standards of professional conduct; a reflection of American ideals and values.

Midlevel Leaders and Ethical Decision Making

Captains. They work where the rubber meets the road. By the time they attend their advanced courses and CAS3 they've already been in the field for four or five years and have a pretty good idea what's going on. They have finely attuned bullshit detectors.

They've had good role models. But they've also seen things that disturb them. And they've all been through the discomfort of making tough ethical decisions in the real world.

We can't just preach to this group. But we can influence them, because they're still in a formative state. They'll listen to us if we listen to them.

So we do.

We listen to their experiences, their concerns, and how they responded. We're still focused on values, but now we're dealing with midlevel leaders who can illuminate the values in light of their experiences. So it's a give-and-take.

They've all had experience with reporting systems, and they're all concerned about pressure to shade the truth. Military reporting systems have to be honest and accurate because our operations are based on them. Unpleasant information can't be suppressed.

That's the theory.

But there's also pressure to embellish. There's a temptation to paint a rosier picture than the unvarnished truth would allow. Sometimes it's signing off on an inflated report prepared by a subordinate. Sometimes it's signing off ahead of time on the assumption you can fix it later.

The rationalizations can be insidious, and in some units, they become the norm.

We make time to talk about these ethical dilemmas, and then we break down situations using the CAS3 problem-solving process. We find that the process works just as well for ethical dilemmas as it does for every other kind of problem. So why not apply it to ethical problems? Here's a sample ethical dilemma.

Situation. You just finished a year as a training officer in a light infantry battalion. The only failure in your tenure was your inability to achieve the standard of a weapons qualification rate of 90 percent. You are now reassigned to the division training directorate. Your first mission is to help select a battalion to take on an important peace enforcement mission. Your new boss tells you the unit must have rock-solid weapons qualification stats. As you look through the various units' statistics, you notice that all ten battalions under consideration have reported achieving the 90 percent standard—including your former battalion! Your former battalion commander calls and mentions that he would really like to have the mission, and that he is still working on your report card.

Define the Problem. No, it's not "how to get the best report card." A better problem statement would be, "To determine the best battalion for the peace enforcement mission." But since in this case we want to focus on the ethical dilemma, we'll go with, "What should I do about false or inaccurate weapons qualification reporting in the light infantry battalion?"

Gather the Facts. The facts are provided, although in working ourselves into the situation we can certainly see where some further fact-finding would be in order. Also, our assumptions will make a big difference in how the situation plays out. For instance, do we assume the battalion commander to be ethical?

Develop Courses of Action. These can become fairly sophisticated, but in raw terms they include:

1. Accept all stats as reported.

2. Report the perceived discrepancy to your former battalion commander.

3. Report the perceived discrepancy to your new supervisor.

Criteria. We'll use evaluation criteria to analyze and compare the courses of action. Again, in simple terms, the criteria might include:

1. Best for the mission.

2. Best for the battalion commander.

3. Best for me.

Obviously the mission is what's most important here. But if we're honest, other considerations are also impacting our responses. We feel loyalty to our former boss, as well as personal concern. We're better off admitting it—and then putting all personal considerations in perspective.

Analyze and Compare the Courses of Action. A careful review of the situation should bring our moral responsibility into sharper focus. While having the report card hanging over our head is daunting, the importance of getting the facts straight and choosing the best battalion must override personal concerns. We'll weight the criteria heavily in favor of "Best for the mission."

Choose the Best Course of Action. Plenty of room for discussion here, and that's what we want. Ethical dilemmas do not often lend themselves to the cut-and-dried; tweaking a fact or nuance can make a big difference in how the situation plays out. In this case, reporting the weapons qualification reporting discrepancy to the former battalion commander is probably the best course of action at this point in the dilemma.

Summary. There are sometimes disturbing issues that come out of this process, but at least we're getting them out in the open and dealing with them. Not only are we shining a light on ethics, we're also reinforcing our problem-solving process and learning about each other as teammates. It's a win-win situation.

★ ★ ★ **STRATEGY 25** ★ ★ ★

USE THE ETHICAL DECISION-MAKING PROCESS. Examine ethical dilemmas for hidden opportunities. Get issues out in the open and deal with them. Watch out for rationalizations; they can be insidious and even become the norm. Define problems. Gather facts. Develop, analyze, and compare courses of action. Do what's right.

Senior Officer Case Studies

You can never take ethics for granted. Even at the top. Leaders have moral failings just like everybody else, with one difference—the fall is farther and the splat is louder. It affects a lot more people. Leadership failures are devastating to an organization.

There are always going to be some senior leaders who almost seem evil. These are the guys who've used unethical methods to get to the top and have perfected the art of covering their tracks. Worst case, these people preach a moral absolutism, and demonstrate the exact opposite. It's tough to work for them.

But more often the problems stem from simply cutting corners. Leaders veer off track one small step at a time, lured by the insidious desire to get ahead. These people are salvageable; we just need to get them to refocus on what's important and prepare them for increased responsibility—and scrutiny.

Senior leaders have less supervision than their subordinates. As they've climbed the ladder they've gained latitude and confidence in their ethical decision making. Some of them pick up the "I am the State" attitude that Louis the XIV demonstrated in eighteenth-century France. The logic goes like this: "I am one with the organization. What's best for me is best for the organization; therefore, I must have the best of everything." It didn't work for Louis XIV, and it doesn't work for military leaders either.

The temptations and responsibilities are different for senior leaders, and it's critical that we prepare them for the challenge. Leaders are responsible for the moral climate in their unit. They're responsible for what happens in their unit. They must be proactive in setting the tone.

Senior leaders are carefully observed by subordinates. Soldiers model their behavior and pick up on their priorities. Actions speak louder than words.

Field grade and general officers need to see the whole playing field when making ethical decisions, because their decisions have a big impact. So we give them case studies to chew on—historical vignettes designed to get their attention. The case studies basically say, "This is the kind of situation in which you could find yourself. What did these guys do right? What did they do wrong? What were the ramifications?"

The case studies are designed to scare the bejesus out of them. Check these out and you'll see what I mean.

My Lai. Angry, frustrated American soldiers are given orders to eliminate an enemy battalion and burn houses, kill livestock, and destroy foodstuffs. They receive no instructions on the safeguarding of noncombatants in the area. What results is the wholesale slaughter of hundreds of innocent civilians, including women and children.

A massive cover-up ensues. Officers throughout the chain of command deliberately conceal the true facts of the crimes committed. Unit investigations are superficial and misleading. It takes a high-level investigation to unearth the facts of the situation.

Lessons Learned. Orders must be clear, and leaders are responsible. Leaders must have a system for communicating their standards and concerns up and down the chain of command. There can be no vacillation with the truth. Leaders must take whatever remedial action is required, regardless of personal consequences.

Yamashita. General Tomoyuki Yamashita was given the mission of commanding Japanese forces in the Philippines in September 1944. During his command, widespread starvation, torture, and general disregard for human life were present in his prison camps. Thousands were summarily executed.

Upon Japanese surrender, General Yamashita was tried by a military tribunal. His case was appealed to the U.S. Supreme Court, which upheld his guilt and the recommended death sentence.

Lessons Learned. U.S. Military Code incorporates the "Yamashita Standard," requiring commanders to take all feasible measures within their power to prevent inhuman acts in their command. Further, they must disseminate knowledge of the laws of war, investigate when necessary, and take appropriate disciplinary actions. Commanders have personal criminal liability for failure to control criminal acts in their command.

Tail Hook. The Tail Hook Association is a private organization, composed primarily of Navy and Marine aviators. Total attendance at their 1991 convention in Las Vegas may have numbered 5,000, although official registration was about 2,000, and included top Navy brass. The conventions had a history of wild partying, but the 1991 convention devolved into an orgy of immoral activity and sexual assault.

Initial Navy investigations attempted to limit the exposure of the Navy and senior Navy officials. Ultimately, the careers of 14 admirals and 300 aviators were damaged or destroyed. The Navy underwent significant cultural change through education and training, and Navy support for the association was eventually restored in 1999.

Lessons Learned. Military organizations don't have the right to carry on unethical traditions. Senior leaders must be finely attuned to situations that could jeopardize their integrity and be proactive in changing moral climates for the better. Accusations of illegal, immoral, or unethical activity must be investigated aggressively and fairly—regardless of the level of the officials who may be impacted.

Summary.   Obviously, reviewing case studies like these is a painful process for senior officers. For each failure, there are many successes when leaders have chosen the hard right over the easy wrong. Heroic choices often go unnoticed.

I've also simplified the case studies. Much more has been said; many more lessons have been learned; and debate still rages on many of the issues.

But you get the idea. And you have to admire an organization that has the courage to try and come to grips with these issues. No pain, no gain.

The Case Study from Hell

Nobody is pitching this case study—it's too hot to handle. And the lessons learned are all the wrong ones.

It seems that one commander in chief of the United States Military had inappropriate sexual relations with a White House intern.

These acts, and this relationship, went against everything we teach in senior-subordinate relationships. We believe the senior person present has the ultimate responsibility for maintaining a professional environment.

The lesson learned is that the same standards that apply to us should also apply to the commander in chief. Otherwise the message is that the Code of Conduct doesn't matter. It's not difficult to imagine a couple of boneheads who say "Hey, the commander in chief did it and kept his job, why can't I?"

★ ★ ★ **STRATEGY 26** ★ ★ ★

UNDERSTAND THERE WILL ALWAYS BE ETHICAL DILEMMAS. Ethical dilemmas don't go away because you're the leader or because you've attained a certain level of enlightenment. In fact, they become more challenging. Leaders set the tone. Subordinates model leader behavior. Be proactive; challenge unethical traditions and reinforce what the team is doing right.

You Can Handle the Truth

The truth often hurts, but you can handle it.

That's what we rediscovered in America's Military after Vietnam. As an organization we chose to do the right thing, because in the long run, in the aggregate, it's better for everyone. Doing the right thing not only builds self-esteem, it's actually a more effective way of getting things done.

When we compared ourselves to our number one adversary, the Soviet Union, we saw they actually had a number of the same values—loyalty, duty, courage. But they lacked integrity. Communist ideology proffered that "the truth is whatever we say it is." The Soviet Union was based on systematic lying. There was no integrity. Ultimately, systems without integrity fail.

To the degree that we institutionalize falsehood, we're slowing progress. I'm not saying we can ever know absolute truth or that anyone purporting to have a corner on the truth is beyond reproach. It's the *quest* for truth that's important—illuminating values, making them come alive, and applying them to the real world.

Morals are like muscles; you have to work them out. It takes commitment and continual striving. Otherwise you just slip back into mediocrity, or worse, go down the slippery slope of expediency. Take nothing for granted. Test everything.

Make ethics a part of your environment—at home and at work. Weave ethical considerations into the fabric of your life.

Don't become obsessed with image. The image freaks will tell you, "It's going to look bad; the truth is too ugly to confront."

Strike a balance between form and substance—that ratio between looking good and being good. They go hand in hand.

Beware of bosses who misuse the loyalty you extend to them, who say one thing but mean something entirely different. Success can be heady, and sometimes the successful come to believe they can bend reality. "It's the truth because I will it to be so," they seem to be saying, "I will state the reality, and you will make it happen."

Beware of "making things happen." Beware of "fix it."

Make things happen. Fix things. But don't give or take orders where the ethics are ambiguous.

The challenge is to make wise ethical decisions when absolutes collide with expediency. Know the values; practice ethical decision making; and think through situations. Then do what's right.

Train Tough Challenge

Watch out for your next ethical dilemma. Break it down; analyze it. Then take the high road to a solution. Do it again on your next dilemma. It takes practice.

———— ★ ————

PART THREE

THE COMBAT
BUSINESS MODEL

The same old stuff. With a twist.
Because business is combat.

9

———★———

ORGANIZATION

The Structure of Success

The primary object of organization is to shield people from unexpected calls upon their powers of adaptability, judgment and decision.
—General Jan Hamilton

War is organized chaos. There's nothing more challenging than organizing chaos, but that's what we do.

The U.S. Military is big on structure, because we know a strong structure will hold us together when the going gets tough.

We're hooked on organization. It's the most underappreciated and misunderstood aspect of our success.

In the old days, a commander was ordered to "organize" a force to accomplish a given mission. That was a tall order. It meant he was responsible for the full spectrum of recruiting, housing, feeding, training, and structuring his force. He had to be organized. We still activate military units with an organization order. Every year units celebrate "Organization Day."

How a unit is structured and organized is a big deal. Every soldier, sailor, airman, or marine is authorized by document, as is every major piece of equipment. The document is reviewed all the way up the chain of command to Washington, D.C. Personnel and equipment requisitions are filled against that authorization document. It's the organization document that keeps a land commander at Fort Riley, Kansas, from ordering a battleship and a couple of submarines.

The planners in the Pentagon see the big picture, tailoring the force to fit the mission. We want to structure ourselves for maximum effectiveness, and that takes strategic design—knowing our adversaries, knowing what's in our inventory, and then getting the force mix just right.

It's easy to take organization for granted, because in the day-to-day hubbub, it's almost invisible. But the wise leader looks beneath the surface, seeing all the way into the structure and organization of things. It's there that success is tailored.

The concept of organization is boring for some people. We like to think we thrive on chaos.

But the reality is, the more chaotic the environment, the greater the need for organization.

Sure, if your life is a breeze, you can swag organization. You can wing it. You can afford to get lost, misplace things, and stumble from task to task. Being disorganized certainly adds to the random chaos of life, and for some it's a necessary stimulant to an otherwise mundane existence.

For some, disorganization is an act of rebellion. Fight the power. Bless this mess.

But the reality is that organization is liberating, not confining. Organization offers the gift of time, and freedom from the tyranny of confusion.

★ ★ ★ **STRATEGY 27** ★ ★ ★

NEVER UNDERESTIMATE THE POWER OF ORGANIZATION. We often take organization for granted. Living in chaos is sometimes our little way to fight the power. Organization seems boring and its processes laborious. But ultimately, organization is liberating. It eliminates confusion and saves precious time. It's an acquired taste.

The U.S. Military System of Organization

At the head of every military unit is the commander, the guy responsible. He's accountable for everything the unit does or fails to do, the guy who makes the big decisions and maintains the vision.

Commanders need a lot of help. The art of command is very much the art of delegation, the business of assigning the right task to the right person. The commander has help even in this—in the form of his executive officer.

If the commander is the leader, the exec is the ultimate manager. When the fit is good, the executive officer can virtually read the mind of the commander, anticipating actions before they take the form of orders.

The executive officer runs the staff, and ultimately the stuff of the unit. The commander inspires; the exec requires. When they're functioning in sync they form the perfect leadership and management team.

Military staffs are organized in similar fashion at every level of the military. A battalion S1, or personnel officer, has counterparts at brigade, division, and corps levels. So, in addition to the command relationships at each level, there are also staff relationships. It's a structure that makes sense.

Staff structure is uniform. An Army battalion in Colorado has the same structure as an Army battalion in Korea. The staff is not something that has to be invented in each unit; the organization is the same wherever you go.

Here's how we're organized.

S1, Personnel. The S1 is the human resources manager, the one who makes sure the right person is getting to the right job. Pay, promotions, and evaluations all fall under the S1. She is also responsible for morale support activities, chaplain and legal services, and the health and welfare of the unit. Safety and accident trends are monitored by the S1, and the results are passed to subordinate units so they get the benefit of lessons learned.

The S1 is the unit's chief administrator, coordinating all procedures in the unit. She is typically authorized to sign documents "For the Commander," an important delegation that relieves the commander from personal involvement in the routine matters of the command.

S2, Intelligence. The S2 acquires intelligence information and data, analyzes and evaluates, and presents assessments to the commander. The goal is to allow the commander to see the entire situation and identify high-value targets on the battlefield.

S3, Operations. If the commander and executive officer make up the brain of the unit, then the S3 is the central nervous system, communicating the plan throughout the organization. The S3 drafts the plan for every operation, and oversees these operations—at the direction of the commander. The S3 also prepares and conducts the training programs requisite to accomplishing each mission.

The S3 is the time manager for the unit. There's never enough time to do everything that needs to be done. We plan it that way. The S3 maintains the unit training calendar, ensuring the various training tasks occur in a logical sequence. The goal is to maximize unit proficiency prior to evaluations, deployments, or battle. It's the S3's job to help the commander determine what needs to be done, and what can be left undone.

S4, Logistics. If anybody has to be organized, it's the S4. She oversees supply, maintenance, and transportation, a daunting task at any level.

The S4 determines supply requirements and then requisitions, stores, and distributes the supplies themselves—everything from beans to bullets.

She plans and coordinates all modes of transportation for personnel, equipment, and supplies and oversees maintenance of unit equipment.

She distributes weapons and ammunition. She allocates fuel and provides food service.

The S4 aggressively keeps track of things. Her goal is to know where everything is, all the time. She inventories; she inspects. She makes sure company commanders sign for equipment and understand that they will be held personally responsible for anything they lose.

The unit doesn't just show up at a given time and place—they convoy. The S4 carefully calculates travel speeds and vehicle intervals. Rest and refueling stops are planned along the way. Recovery teams respond to accidents and breakdowns. Every vehicle has a load plan, a detailed sketch of where everything is stored. And every vehicle has a trained driver and a vehicle commander—there's always someone in charge, right up to the convoy commander.

The only way the S4 survives is by ruthless organization, and relentless attention to detail.

★ ★ ★ STRATEGY 28 ★ ★ ★

BEGIN ORGANIZATION WITH PLANNING. Think of a submarine, where the physical construction is predicated on mission, and equipment and personal effects are micro-organized. Everything is labeled and idiot-proofed. The kid who couldn't put his toys away becomes a master organizer on a submarine. He learns to fit into the overall plan.

Summary. OK, I admit it. Discussing staff functions is boring.

The key is to understand the division of labor. If you can see similar elements in your business or organization, you can divide them up—and presto!—you've got a concept for organization.

Organizing for Submarine Warfare

Boarding a Los Angeles–class fast-attack submarine is the ultimate object lesson in naval organization. Where else would you find 152 guys crammed into the living space of a three-bedroom house, with one washer and dryer?

And these guys aren't there for an overnight. The USS *Portsmouth,* which I visited recently, can easily submerge for a month at a time, and remain at sea far longer than that.

The *Portsmouth* is a nuclear-powered killing machine, designed to harass enemy subs and surface ships. It carries a mix of twenty-eight torpedoes and Tomahawk missiles.

Its $1.65 billion price tag includes few creature comforts for the crew. Bunks are either stacked four high or nestled down among the missiles and torpedoes. Exercise facilities consist of the ever-present pipes for doing chin-ups.

"Personal articles properly stowed," listed as one of the captain's *Ten Commandments of Damage Control,* is perhaps the easiest to follow.

"I bring two weeks' worth of socks, T-shirts, and underwear," a crew member told me, "that and a few toiletries pretty well fills up my space." His space consists of a six-inch-deep storage drawer beneath his bunk, known as a "bedpan."

He shows it to me. It is remarkably well organized, each cubbyhole fitted with an essential item, and no more. The orderliness is quite unlike anything I have seen in a college dorm.

"Cleanliness—A direct reflection of pride in ourselves and our ship," reads a sign nearby, another reminder that I am not in a dorm. It is every mother's dream.

The *Portsmouth* is an exhibit of minimalism and simplicity. Small is better here, and less is more. From the width of slender mattresses to the size of a stool, everything is downsized. The submariners themselves tend to be leaner and more compact than their surface counterparts.

Space is planned down to the cubic inch. It's not a question of where to put things, but of what's essential.

Physical layout is predicated on mission, not crew comfort. Even the captain's work area would be cause for an employee grievance on terra firma.

Equipment is micro-organized. Personnel files consist of a single drawer.

Everything is labeled and idiotproofed. "Access to back of clothes dryer," reads one hatch. Lock wires protect the intake valves.

The captain's tenth commandment of damage control serves as the final challenge for the sub's organization: *Know your way around, even in the dark.*

★ ★ ★ **STRATEGY 29** ★ ★ ★

REMEMBER STTP. You've got to organize Stuff, Time and Tasks, People. The more you have, the more you have to organize. Keep it simple. To find time, break it into small segments. Do the same with tasks. Then put the segments in order and prioritize. Keep a to-do list—and a "nudge list" for subordinates. Delegate whenever a subordinate can do a routine task with 75 percent proficiency.

Operation Organization

Organization is a learned skill. Some people develop a knack for it, so in that sense it's like anything else. But whether you have the knack or not, it's a skill you need in your inventory. Without organization, you're going to be reinventing the obvious over and over again, expending precious energy and adding friction to your life.

Organization begins with planning, built on a certain amount of knowledge. Yes, it helps if you know what you're doing. But even if you don't, an organized approach to learning is still superior. You just adjust as you go. That's what a plan is anyway, a sort of map that you can follow—or digress from as you see fit. At least with a plan you know where you are and where you turned off the road.

The acronym for organization is STTP—Stuff, Time and Tasks, People. We have plenty of acronyms in the military, to the point where they've become a coded language unto themselves. But they can be useful shortcuts to express thoughts or to remember a series of thoughts.

In essence, STTP covers all the areas of an organized military staff. Let's take them one at a time.

Stuff. Stuff is anything physical—furniture, a screwdriver, a piece of paper. It makes up the clutter of our lives. We acquire things for a buzz of some sort and very often live with a drone of overabundance for the rest of our lives.

The first rule of stuff is simplicity. If you're surrounded by more than you need, you've created a job for yourself—managing the stockyard. Most of us aren't very good at that job, and the result is a mess.

Acquisition is a habit, reinforced by a culture of competition and consumption. Don't get me wrong, I like it here. The system works. But the pressure to acquire is insidious, and runs counter to good organization.

Develop buyer resistance, casting a critical eye on your purchase temptations.

Even if the price is low, is it something you'll ever use? What's the storage cost?

Will the new toaster fit in the cabinet? Will the new VCR balance on top of the new TV? If we're honest, most purchases are letdowns. We bring the acquisition home, only to be disappointed or quickly jaded. And we build up clutter.

Take a thirty-day moratorium on all capital purchases, a cold-turkey statement of control. Stop the buying. Find things not to like about what you don't have. Create a mood. The economy can survive without you for a while.

Organize what you have. Sell or donate what you don't need. It's not just a question of where to put something, but whether you will use the item at all. Err on the side of discarding. Remember, you're paying a psychic storage fee for what you keep.

Design a system so you know where everything is, all the time. Organize like a submariner.

Label boxes and file folders.

Secure valuables.

Arrange. Design your physical layout to send the messages you wish to convey. Your office should convey professionalism. Your home should convey flow and warmth.

Maintain an organized mind-set as you work. Organization is a learned skill.

Time and Tasks. There's considerable debate in the military about whether we manage time or tasks. The two are inextricably linked.

But let's begin with time, the great equalizer. Everyone gets twenty-four hours to their day. It's standard issue, like air. Some of us do a great deal in twenty-four hours, while others find unique ways to squander this precious resource. The gift is the same for everyone; we all use it or lose it in different ways.

Time is wealth.

Who's wealthier, Warren Buffett with his billions or a nineteen-year-old in perfect health? Whose remaining life would you choose? It's a tough question, because of our tendency to underestimate the value of time.

Regain an appreciation for time by breaking it into segments. Cubby-hole it like a submariner's storage area.

Give yourself eight hours for sleep. Then start with your wake-up routine and move through your morning activities all the way to work.

Analyze your workday and the rhythm of the week. Find your high-energy periods and schedule high-value tasks for those times. Identify down periods for potential renovation, whereby you replace time-wasting activities with higher-value activities, like exercise.

Take control of your calendar. Look out five years and reverse plan to the next twenty minutes.

One of the great things about time is that, while we can learn from the past and imagine the future, we experience time only in the present moment. We set up the quality of the present moment through planning—and that means taking control of our calendars and schedules.

Organization leads to freedom, the time to do what we all crave as human beings—absolutely nothing. "Absolutely nothing" is like a vitamin. We need it in just the right dosage, not too much, not too little.

Managing time means handling distractions and mastering your anti-interruption tactics.

Be ruthless with a heart.

Be ruthless with the stupid stuff you've allowed yourself to slip into, like off-the-track conversations with coworkers. But be sensitive to the needs of family members who need access and a sounding board. Most of these judgment calls are obvious; it just takes focus to begin executing what you know and feel.

Skim when you read. Take control of the phone. Master the art of e-mail.

Develop a sense of timing as you move into tasks.

What's important? When are you at your best?

I try to do projects in the morning and interact with people in the afternoon. My mind is sharpest and my energy highest right after breakfast.

That's my focus time. People tend to energize me, so I often get my second wind by interacting socially in the afternoon. It may be different for you.

Most tasks become more difficult with age, like reconstructing trip reports or publishing the minutes of a meeting. It's critical to knock out these kinds of tasks immediately, as they become exponentially more complicated as time passes. Memory fades and notes grow stale.

Break big jobs into small pieces, and prioritize their accomplishment.

For complex projects use the critical path method, whereby pivotal tasks are identified and given a high priority. In the military we lay out all the tasks that must be accomplished in the order in which they must be accomplished. Then we look for the "key nodes," those critical tasks that will impact the entire project. We refer to a key node as "the long pole in the tent," because if we don't put the long pole in at just the right time and place, we have to undo the work already done, and start over.

Track your tasks with a prioritized to-do list. Monitor the progress of subordinates with a "nudge list," a semipublic list of the projects you consider important with the name of the responsible individual clearly identified with each project. It won't be the most popular tracking system, but it will challenge people to get things done.

Take control of paperwork. Digitize to the max. Keep your desk clear. Have the goal of handling each piece of paper only once. File it, delegate it, deal with it, or trash it.

Keep a notebook or use a PDA. As a lieutenant, I kept track of things on scraps of paper, but as a captain it was notebook time. A small notebook is essential for keeping your calendar, task list, and other vital information. There's lots of new technology in this arena.

People. People are a two-edged sword, both an asset and a liability. Success depends on how you leverage this important resource.

You've got to make time for friends, customers, and family. Not to mention supervisors, subordinates, and coworkers. It's another question of strategy and tactics.

But rather than get into a sensitive area, let me just be insensitive. You can add sensitivity as desired. I'll boil it down to two points.

One. Deal with problem children. In the workplace, that sometimes means directing them to a new career—somewhere else. As the Navy would say, *blow ballast*—the deadweight that causes you to take on water, the 10 percent of the people who cause 90 percent of the problems, the 20 percent of the people who take up 80 percent of a conversation. Hey, it's a whitewater world. You can't save everybody, but you can die trying. Be creative in how you blow ballast. It's an art form.

Two. Delegate. If you're in a position to delegate, then delegation is part of your job. If you don't have enough time, you're not delegating. If subordinates can do the job to 75 percent of your proficiency, let them do it. If you're doing their job, you're not doing yours.

Delegation is good for you and good for them. Delegation develops people, both the delegator and the delegated upon. It's part of supervision, and part of being a subordinate who takes care of the boss.

There is a certain ethic to delegation. Sitting on a project and then delegating at the sound of the buzzer is bad form. Otherwise, the sky's the limit. When you have someone handling your delegation for you, you'll know you've mastered the craft.

OK. Now add the sensitivity.

Train Tough Challenge

Think big. In the following space, organize how you're going to organize. Think through how you're going to stay organized.

_____

_____

_____

10

★

EXECUTION

The Art and Science of High Performance

Let no man feel he is tired so long as he can put one foot in front of the other. Demand the impossible in order that the possible may be accomplished.

—General Charles Summerall

Until now I've resisted the urge to use sports analogies, which is difficult because I played sports throughout my military career. Sports are a big part of who I am and how I think.

It's hard to talk about execution and high performance without thinking of sports. For me, it's unavoidable. I'll try to get most of it out of my system in this chapter.

The focus of this chapter is execution; in sports terms, we're talking about carrying the ball.

What do you do when you're handed the ball?

Stand there?

Drop it?

Or run like hell?

We've all had the experience in life and in our careers of being handed the ball. Sometimes it seems as if there's no plan and nobody blocking. In football we call it a broken play. You've still got to take the ball and run it up the field.

As a leader I got good at picking soldiers I could hand the ball in tough situations—guys who knew where the goal was and which direction to run. They knew how to protect the football, and would do everything in their power to advance it. They were players. Performers.

Other guys you'd hand the ball and they'd say, "What's this? If I take this, somebody's going to hit me."

And they'd cough it up. Or stand around waiting for instructions.

Down they'd go.

There are several structures that support high performance. Organization. Preparation. Teamwork.

But this chapter is about grasping the football and running down the field.

It's about getting hit, breaking tackles, and hanging onto the ball.

It's about the difference between putting points on the board or fumbling the ball to the other fellow.

Execution. Performance. That's what this chapter is about.

Gulf War II

The off-the-shelf plan for Operation Iraqi Freedom called for 500,000 troops. The Americans and Brits accomplished the mission with about a third that number.

It was a new kind of coalition warfare, a quantum leap forward from Desert Storm, fought just twelve years before.

We had special forces in the west capturing Scud missiles before they could be launched, special forces helping the Kurds in the north, and a rock 'n' roll conventional invasion in the south.

There was no thirty-day preparatory bombardment as in Desert Storm. Precision-guided bombs, using lasers and global positioning satellites, greatly reduced the number of sorties flown as well as the number of civilian casualties.

We took out the enemy's command-and-control network early on; first he lost control of the Republican Guard, then situational awareness, then all touch with reality. The surreal performance of the Iraqi information minister denying Allied success as we rolled into Baghdad was priceless.

The ground race to Baghdad never slowed to defend flanks. Special forces blew up bridges the Iraqis needed to attack from the flank, and our air attacks destroyed the enemy while he tried to figure out what to do next. Special forces picked a lightly defended route into Baghdad and secured the bridges we crossed to get there. Our mechanized infantry arrived before the bad guys had time to set up a defense.

We could observe, decide, execute, and assess far faster than the enemy. The teamwork between our allies and our Army, Navy, Air Force, and Marines was exceptional—assisted by an ultramodern command post with state-of-the-art technology. Commanders had a clear picture of the battlefield, viewing air frames, ships, and ground units in real time—while conversing via videoconference.

Transformed by digital technology, our logistics supply was three times faster and more efficient than twelve years prior. Radio transmitter tags tracked when and where supplies would arrive. Logistics reach was greatly extended, with combat units and supply convoys linked by transponders.

The pressure on the Iraqis was relentless. Speed and firepower, leveraging cutting-edge technology, was decisive.

Gulf War II was a testament to individual soldiers, sailors, airmen, and marines executing a plan with skill and tenacity. In difficult weather and terrain they performed brilliantly. Ultimately, wars are still won by small unit tactical skill and the courage of every person on the team.

A good plan. Training that puts a premium on high performance. Execution and hard work. That's what it takes.

The Psychology of High Performance

One of the goals of a figure skater is to make movement look effortless, to create a sense of confidence and wonder. She'll work long hours to create this magical effect. It takes a lot of work to make it look easy.

We often lose sight of this simple concept. We resist the work. We procrastinate. We whine and snivel, building up angst and frustration as the tasks mount and grow more daunting.

We need to get our minds right.

Very few accomplishments occur without hard work. More often, the quality of an end product is directly proportional to the work invested. Whether it's a successful party or a sales presentation, hard work is always in there somewhere. There's no escaping it.

You have to embrace the work.

As a coach, I tell my teams we will not be outworked. We will know, every time we step out on the field or court, that we have outworked our competition. We will have worked harder and smarter. We will therefore deserve to win. We can claim victory in advance because we have already done the work. As we move into the execution phase of the actual game, we have a feeling of ownership, that the game belongs to us and that we are warding off usurpers, people trying to take what is rightfully ours. The right attitude about our work investment gives us the psychological upper hand. We deserve to win.

Work is not a dirty word. In fact, the need to work is a key component of the human psyche; it's part of what makes us complete as human beings.

Our capacity for work is deepened through practice and training. It's like physical fitness—it develops through exercise. It hurts a little at first, but gradually we master the process by consistent effort. And we build confidence.

I'm not talking drudgery for the sake of drudgery here. I'm talking about drudgery with a purpose.

One of my jobs as a coach is to turn work into play. I don't want to take a bored, burned-out team into competition. In fact, my goal is to never bore or burn out my team at any point in the process. Just the opposite! The challenge of the coach is to dole out the drudgery in acceptable doses, wedged between activities that excite and invigorate.

Yes, we drill. But we drill only to the point of saturation, when momentary mastery is achieved and the first hint of euphoria kicks in. Then we move to something else. We always leave them wanting more.

Ultimately, the psychology of work leads back to that simple question: "How bad do you want it?"

If you're not sure of the answer, maybe you're in the wrong business or career field. Maybe you're in a situation that's sapping your desire instead of feeding it. Maybe it's time to move on to something that will light your fire.

There's a one-word answer to the "How bad do you want it?" question; it's "*bad.*"

When you want something bad enough, you're willing to do the work—to do the hard work that victory demands. You're on your way to becoming an achiever.

Some folks may say this is all too much effort, that we need to let go and let the universe take its course, that we're already too results oriented and stressed out.

I partially agree.

There is a time to let go and let nature take its course.

The problem is that too many people put this piece at the beginning of the task and never get beyond it. They never get to the work. They've let go with nothing to grab onto. They're drifting.

The key is to know when to bear down and when to let go.

There's a time for both.

Finding the right work is very often the product of letting go, of getting in touch with our inner selves and our deep desires.

But when we find the right work it's time to get to work. Once we hear the calling it's time to rock and roll, to execute, to perform.

When we've done the work, we can let go again, secure in the knowledge that we've done our best.

I call this the "no regrets" philosophy. Do your best. The results will follow. How can you have regrets when you've done your best?

The successful figure skater is relaxed because, after all the hard work, she's let go. She's no longer concerned about the competition, the judges, or the risk of failure. She's lost in the moment, the supreme moment of execution.

High performance is the result of preparation, execution, and assessment. Everybody wants to win, but only champions have the will to prepare.

★ ★ ★ STRATEGY 30 ★ ★ ★

UNDERSTAND THE PSYCHOLOGY OF HIGH PERFORMANCE. Superior performance is attained by people who love what they're doing. It can also be generated by necessity. Embrace the work. Commit to never being outworked. Adopt a "no regrets" philosophy, the idea that you're going to do your best and let the chips fall where they may. It takes a lot of work to make it look easy.

Preparation

"Bender, you are not arriving to battle at the decisive time and place."

Those words stung, but I had to admit the man was right. And there's nothing like hearing that kind of assessment from the boss. It was time to take stock.

Yes, I was executing, but I was focused on the close-in battle, killing bad guys as they leapt over the top of my desk. And you can't win major battles when you're tied up in hand-to-hand combat. You've got to assess what your role is in the big picture and then play to that level. Hire somebody to provide security and take care of the little problems. Or delegate.

High-performance execution is choosing, and then winning, the right battles. Fighting every fight is called a brawl. You've got to be more organized than that.

The preparatory phase of execution is tremendously important. That's when you determine what to do, how to do it, and how bad you want to get it done. It's where you plan, rehearse, and establish the vision of how you'll attack the situation. Let's think through the components of preparation.

Decide. Pick your battles. True, some battles are going to pick you. But to the maximum extent possible you want to set up your life so you're fighting the battles that will make a difference, executing on what's important. You want to compete in situations that make maximum use of your particular skills and talents. Hire or delegate in those areas that don't interest you or don't take optimum advantage of your skill set.

Look before you leap. Once in a while you have to climb the mountain, get away from the fighting, and look down on the battlefield for a better perspective. Observe. See where you can make a difference, then throw yourself back into the fray.

Commit. Observe, decide, commit. Commitment is critical, sometimes even more important than precisely what was decided upon. Success is determined by the level of commitment. An imperfect plan improves with tenacity.

Accept responsibility for your decisions—head and heart. Wandering onto the battlefield will only get you killed. Establish the mind-set of making things work. Commit to high performance.

Construct. Build a plan of attack, and tie the plan to your overall strategy. Sequence operations using reverse planning. See your plan from front to back, and from back to front. Quantify the time and energy required. Plan to work hard, but factor in rest periods as well.

Look for synergy with all your assets. Leverage technology. Understand yourself and human nature as it applies to those who will assist you. Build in accountability and make it part of the reward system.

Rehearse. Even the Normandy invasion was rehearsed. The Allies encountered many problems in rehearsal, even losing some men, but they were far better off when they executed the real thing under fire.

Practice doesn't always make perfect, but perfect practice comes pretty close. You won't see the shortcomings in your plan until you run through it in practice. And what you find in practice can be fixed. Better in practice than in the execution phase.

Visualize how you want things to go. See yourself performing, adapting to situations as they arise. Program yourself for success. You've done the work. You deserve to win.

Execution

This is where preparation pays off. You've chosen your battle, committed to it, built a plan, and rehearsed. It's time to move out.

Execution is about fundamentals, making maximum use of that professional skill set you've internalized. Regardless of how complicated the task, never lose sight of the basics. They will hold you in good stead when the going gets tough.

Now it's all about performance.

Perform. Take the ball and run. Get off to a good start. Expect the unexpected, and run anyway.

Focus. Adapt. Work through the pain, that sweet agony of excellence. It's unavoidable. Work through friction—fatigue, complications, lack of time, all the things that go wrong. Keep a can-do attitude. Find a way to win.

Maintain situational awareness. Don't be surprised to be surprised. Stay in the moment.

Success comes with prolonged concentration. Stay committed, willing to do whatever it takes to achieve your mission.

Communicate. We've found in the military that we can accomplish just about anything if everybody knows the play and knows where the enemy is. We've worked very hard to that end.

Push information to your people and your family. Suck it out of your support systems and pass it along to those who need it.

Coordinate. Assume nothing, except that team members won't get the message unless you pass it to them.

Finish Strong. The last 10 percent of any job or project is always the toughest and often the most important. How often do we see a building project stuck on "almost finished"? Everything's done except the final touches that drag on for months.

Attend to these kinds of details, don't let them keep you from completion.

Since you've reverse-planned the mission, you know what these final elements are and have allocated time and energy for their completion.

Persevere to the end. It's always too soon to quit.

Assess. Assessment should be continuous, like a homing device that directs to the target—a series of tiny adjustments that keep you on track.

But sometimes the situation calls for a more formal assessment, such as an after-action report—a succinct and incisive product that details the result of battle for those who follow.

Either way, make learning a continuous process.

★ ★ ★   **STRATEGY 31**   ★ ★ ★

ALWAYS BE PREPARED. Pick your battles carefully. Then commit. Build a plan, one that creates the best synergy for the assets available. Visualize. Rehearse. Don't be surprised to be surprised.

Celebrate Everything

I've come to a couple of conclusions about teams. One is that there are basically two kinds of organizations: those that celebrate everything, and those that celebrate nothing.

The second is that it's a heck of a lot more fun to be a part of organizations that celebrate everything.

Celebration is an attitude. It's contagious.

The best sports teams I played on were usually the ones that had a beer roster. Win, lose, or draw, we had a couple of beers after the game. We celebrated our exploits and bonded.

Contrast that with a boss I had who bought a fancy bottle of liquor and kept it behind his desk. Someday we were going to "celebrate." Someday never came.

People need to feel rewarded. They need to unwind.

Sure, there are health and safety issues, but these can be worked through.

Work hard. Prepare. Execute like a commando. Then celebrate.

High-Performance Presentations

Let's take the high-performance formula and apply it to one of life's great challenges: the oral presentation. Surveys show that Americans rank public speaking right up there with death as a fear factor.

We do a lot of oral presentations in the military; we call them briefings. "Brief me" can mean anything from a thirty-second rundown to a three-hour dog and pony show. We have information briefings and decision briefings, informal and formal settings. Regardless of venue, it's all about knowing your stuff and being able to communicate it.

I delivered a lot of briefings in my career and critiqued many hundreds as an instructor. I found that while some people have a natural gift for communicating with an audience, almost anyone can develop this important talent. But it takes a system.

Preparation. Many times you don't have a choice of venue for a presentation; that decision is made for you. It's important to learn as much as you can about the situation—the audience, expectations, and setting. Get an idea of how much time you'll have.

Commit to doing the work that high performance demands. Getting motivated shouldn't be difficult. We're often judged on how we perform in this important arena, so see it as an opportunity to shine—and get your message out at the same time.

Constructing your presentation is where the real work is. You're going to have to think. There's no way around it.

Start with how much time you'll have. If you have latitude, always err on the side of brevity. "Be brief, be brilliant, be gone" is a motto that has served me well.

Keep it simple. Start with the main points you want to make. Don't reach too far. Winston Churchill said an audience can digest only two or three main points.

Once you've selected these main points, research the details you'll need to communicate your message.

Keep an eye out for the tough issues. Many times we're asked to speak on an issue because the situation is thorny to begin with. There's no substitute for thoroughly knowing your subject when this is the case. Just do the work.

As your presentation takes form, consider visual aids. In general, the stronger your presentation skills, the less is the need for visuals. On the other hand, you may be presenting in an environment where visuals are expected, or where you know other presenters will be using them with great effect. You make the call, but again err on the side of simplicity.

Make sure you thoroughly understand any statistics you present, and make sure you can handle any technological demands. You don't want to be ambushed by technical difficulties.

Rehearse! Run through your presentation from start to finish. As you do, you'll notice the rough spots and danger areas and be able to adjust accordingly. Time yourself. Execute gestures and facial expressions as if it were the real thing.

If possible, practice your presentation in the exact location where you will deliver it. Tailor notes to the situation. You can use large notepaper at a podium, but don't encumber yourself otherwise.

Have a friend or coworker critique you or, better yet, videotape the rehearsal. Many times eliminating one or two annoying habits can make for a vastly improved presentation. You may have a nervous physical tic or be punctuating with "ahs" or "ums" and not even be aware of it.

Polish your opening and closing lines. Know the exact words you'll use. Be able to say these lines without notes, with confidence and effect.

Anticipate questions that may be asked. Formulate answers in advance.

Execution. The good news about execution is that you've already done the work. The hard part is over. All you have to do now is perform with the confidence you've earned.

Before you present, jot down a few notes about what you learned in rehearsal. Find a quiet place to review the notes. Take a few moments to see yourself in your mind's eye—presenting confidently and professionally, to a friendly, interested audience.

Be assured that you can carry this attitude into the real thing. You've done the work!

Afterward, assess how you did. From experience I can tell you that there's almost always something you didn't anticipate—a question, a problem, or a curveball of some kind. I'm rarely completely satisfied with my presentations.

That's just the nature of the beast.

That's life with high standards.

The fact of the matter is that your presentation went very, very well. The little glitches you saw were unseen by the audience. What they saw was a consummate professional who knew her stuff.

So celebrate success.

★ ★ ★ STRATEGY 32 ★ ★ ★

FINISH STRONG. Take the ball and run with it. Maintain situational awareness. Focus. Adapt. Communicate. Run through the finish line, and be sure and set that line out far enough to encompass all the tasks that must be completed. The last 10 percent of any job is always the toughest, usually because nobody planned for it.

Do It Now—or Pay Later

It was an unseasonably warm February, and a soggy one too. I could see there were moles working on the backyard, but I really didn't think much about it. Maybe I really wasn't thinking at all.

Then they hit the front yard like Nazis attacking Russia. They were everywhere, lining the drive and sidewalks, tunneling along the foundation of the house.

I had poisoned the little bastards a few years before, but this time they were poison resistant.

I tried smoking them out, and then drowning them. Each time I claimed victory, they came back with a vengeance. I could kill a bunch of them, but they'd reproduce and come back stronger.

I thought about calling an exterminator; heck, I thought about calling the National Guard.

By midsummer the tide had turned, a tribute to my tenacity and improved methodology. I was a killing machine, mixing high explosives with smoke, poison, flash flooding, and traps. Finally, I was executing. A hard-won peace descended on the yard.

Then in one brutal counterattack it all crumbled. A gopher picked up where the moles left off—just moved right into the abandoned tunnels.

Supergopher was bigger, tougher, and more destructive—cutting large swaths across the front yard, leaving piles of dirt in his wake. Worse, he seemed indestructible.

Then one afternoon while playing basketball with the boys I noticed one of his tunnels visibly advancing. We moved quickly to seal it off.

What happened next is beyond my powers of description. It all boiled down to hand-to-hand combat, in a grisly, torturous war of wills. It was him or me. Without allies and the tenacity born of desperation, I might not have made it. None of us who fought that day will ever be the same.

The healing process continues. The drive and sidewalks all sank several inches, and the ravages of time and climate continue to work on the abandoned tunnels. It's not a pretty sight.

I can't help but reflect how different this story might have been. Sure, there was much to be proud of and a lot of heroism displayed. But what if I had simply taken action on that first warm February morn? How much pain and suffering would have been averted?

Today Operation Mole Watch protects our yard with a steadfast vigilance, ready to respond at a moment's notice to the first sign of trouble. We've moved beyond procrastination and denial. We realize now that we live in a dangerous world where evil rodents will take advantage of any weakness.

Mole Watch has become a metaphor for the penalties of procrastination, a terrible reminder that the most important part of execution is simply getting started.

Train Tough Challenge

List three projects where you've procrastinated, and state why.

1. _____

2. _____

3. _____

Pick one of the three and commit to accomplishing it. Finish strong!

_____

11

---★---

TEAMWORK
With the Emphasis on Work

The Marines have a way of making you afraid—not of dying, but of not doing your job.
—First Lieutenant Bonnie Little

I was tired, just going through the motions of a night patrol. My squad of six men slipped through friendly lines into No-Man's-Land, never bothering to consider how we would return in the pitch darkness without being cut down by our own men.

Our mission was to eavesdrop on the enemy, locate his positions, and estimate his strength. Instead, we walked into an ambush.

A squad member and I advanced to the edge of the enemy encampment. We could see a machine gun and several crates of ammo. Then all hell broke loose. Miraculously, no one from the squad was hit, and we hightailed it out of there.

About halfway back the captain appeared. "Cadet Bender," he said, "you are relieved of your command. Cadet Kowalkski—take over."

I was devastated. It was only a summer camp training exercise and we were all firing blanks, but I knew I had let down the team. In the real thing my incompetence could have gotten us all killed.

Not only had I failed to communicate with friendly forces at the checkpoint, but once I rejoined my squad with critical information about the enemy, I failed to share that information. Had I been killed, the information we had risked our lives for would have been lost. It was a lesson I would relearn again and again and again throughout my military career in a myriad of permutations: Teamwork is built on communication.

I've worked that night patrol through my mind many times. We had been trained in night patrolling and reconnaissance procedures throughout the day. I had probably been picked to lead the patrol because one of the cadre noticed I wasn't paying attention. But I still could have recovered if I had leveraged the knowledge of my team.

Prior to moving out I could have met with squad members, individually and as a group. Together we could have brainstormed the situation and formulated a plan. Woulda. Coulda. Shoulda.

It was easier to sleepwalk into failure.

Teamwork is work. Communication is work. Nothing about it is easy, which is why it yields such great rewards.

If you think about it, it's almost impossible to overcommunicate. I'm not talking about blabbermouthing, spam, or the overbearing boss. I'm talking about communicating.

Nine times out of ten, communication problems are "lack of" as opposed to overload. Overload is a sifting problem; silence is the great unknown. You never know what you don't know.

Teams are built on effective communication, information that is pushed out of one source and pulled into another. A good team member pushes information to the team, and pulls information from other team members. It's a lot of work, but it pays off.

If you feel as if it's you against the world, it's probably because you're not communicating. Somewhere along the line you decided that isolation is easier than teamwork. And you were right. The problem is, it's not very effective.

Let me put it this way: If everybody on your team knew what was going on, you'd be halfway to mission accomplishment. Half the job is getting your team on the same page.

If everybody knew the plan, the issues, current actions, and what the competition was up to, you'd be way ahead.

But it's hard. Teamwork is hard, hard work.

★ ★ ★ STRATEGY 33 ★ ★ ★

GET YOUR TEAM ON THE SAME PAGE. Half of any job is communication. Everybody thinks they communicate, but they don't. Communication is work; it's not easy. You have to push and pull information—pull it out of sources and push it out to your people. When everybody knows the plan, the issues, current actions, and what the competition is up to, you'll be halfway home.

The Allies and World War II: The Advantage of Megateaming

The Germans and Japanese were formidable enemies of freedom in World War II. They both got off to a hot start, fighting fanatically and effectively. They were great bullies—brimming with confidence while committing strategic mistakes that would lead to their mutual downfall. They had common goals and proclaimed themselves allies, but they were never really a team.

The Germans and Japanese fought separate wars, unable to bridge their geographic and cultural divides and hammer out a common strategy. Not only was Hitler surprised by the Japanese attack on Pearl Harbor, his staff officers had trouble locating Hawaii on the map for him. That's how unco-ordinated their efforts were.

How well alliances perform during war is largely a function of team-work. How leaders lead, whether the truth can be told, and how nations communicate are a big part of success or failure.

The situation at the start of the war was difficult for the United States and Britain, hinging on the relationship between Roosevelt and Churchill, forged during the Battle of Britain. Roosevelt, in opposition to some of the military staff, believed that the British could survive the German onslaught and encouraged them to do so, both spiritually and in the pro-vision of arms and supplies. British perseverance became the stuff of leg-end.

But with U.S. entrance into the war came strategic collision. While both allies agreed on major objectives, there were differences in their approach to the conflict.

The British, reflecting on their losses in World War I's ground warfare and the historic success of their maritime strategies, favored an indirect approach.

The Americans, with bountiful resources and superior numbers, favored an early concentration of overwhelming power against the Germans.

Only through the hard-fought give-and-take of teamwork were these differences resolved. When national interests diverged, they were pains-takingly reconciled. Open communication was key.

Eisenhower, the Allied Commander in Europe, was able to work through the difficult strategic choices with Churchill on the basis of admi-ration and respect—as well as the growing power of the United States and the consistent backing of President Roosevelt. Ego management was a major endeavor throughout the war, between Britain's Montgomery and General Patton in Europe, and MacArthur and Nimitz in the Pacific.

In the end it was the immensity of Allied resources coupled with our ability to work as a team that yielded success. The Germans and Japanese made strange bedfellows, never really in sync on grand strategy, never able to tell the truth to each other, much less communicate.

Teamwork was often painful for the Allies, but eventually it won the day.

Team Building and Aircraft Carriers

Its flight deck is the size of a small farm, four and a half acres. With four engines powered by two nuclear reactors, it cruises at over thirty knots— that's almost thirty-five miles per hour for landlubbers. Four catapults launch its seventy-plus tactical aircraft.

The aircraft carrier USS *John C. Stennis,* commissioned in 1995, can quickly change the dynamic of a dicey situation, demonstrating American resolve and power in a crisis.

The air wing can engage enemy aircraft, ships, submarines, and land targets—and lay mines hundreds of miles from the ship. Its mission is to conduct air strikes, support land battles, protect friendly shipping, and enforce blockades.

The *Stennis* recently returned to port in San Diego after a long deployment in support of Operation Provide Enduring Freedom, supporting operations in Afghanistan. Hopefully, the cooks are getting some time off. Its 5,000-person crew consumes 18,600 meals a day. That's better than three squares a day for some crew members.

Touring the *Stennis* is a lesson in teamwork and communication. From the thumbs-up a pilot gives to signal readiness for takeoff, to the alarm system in the pilothouse, to the color and placement of the flight deck markings, the USS *Stennis* is a study in redundant communication—the capability to pass and receive information through more than one source. Phones are everywhere. The flight deck is videomonitored.

The *Stennis* is well prepared for worst-case scenarios. It can knock down enemy aircraft with a surface-to-air missile system and defend against cruise missile attack with rapid-fire 20-mm guns. The ship has extensive onboard repair capabilities and an onboard hospital. It's a self-contained city, the crew trained in multiple tasks.

And a carrier doesn't sail until her crews are qualified.

The Fleet Training Center San Diego offers some of the most animated team training in the world. It's all here: navigation, electronics, weaponry, surface rescue, microrepair—right down to laundry and food service, and a sixteen-chair student barbershop.

But it's damage control team training that really ratchets up the intensity.

The Navy has two enemies—fire and flood—and its crews must be unwaveringly confident in their ability to stand up to both.

From a distance, wet team training sounds a lot like entering a public swimming pool during free swim. A lot of shouting and spraying. But in fact it's a giant simulator and there's a method to the madness.

Teams are shoring, plugging, patching, or pumping—responding to the commands of the team leader, who shouts to be heard over the roar of rushing water. They don't call it wet training for nothing. Bulkhead holes are plugged, pipes are patched, water is pumped, and the simulated ship structure is shored up, all by a crew performing knee high in rising water—12,000 gallons of it. It looks and sounds very much like the real thing. Before they qualify, teams will respond to a number of computer-driven scenarios. The confidence the teams build here will go with them aboard ship.

Fire is the other hazard.

Here again the teams train in live fire scenarios. There are fire simulators for deck, mess, and berthing compartments.

Training is animated as crews quickly don fireproof suits to take on a deck fire. A dummy pilot roasts in the cockpit as a ball of fire engulfs the aircraft. The hoses open up. The fire is subdued and the pilot evacuated.

Firefighting crews qualify as a team and undergo periodic recertification, for which they receive extra pay. To become a good nozzleman is the goal of every team member, and they take turns at the position.

"It's easy to wear out the nozzleman," a team member tells me, "so the team leader keeps track, and makes sure he rotates out."

"And the role of team in all this training?" I ask a petty officer.

"It's all team," she answers curtly, and she's right. The world's finest navy still invests in teamwork.

Number One in the Nation

She was onstage, completely at ease, funny, with all the poise of a general officer. Major Therese Carmack was one of many presenters at a local high school awards assembly, but she stood out. Afterward, we did some catching up. It had been six years since we served together; she was a captain at the time.

Major Carmack is now the enrollment officer for the Army ROTC Battalion at Central Missouri State University in Warrensburg, Missouri—recently selected the top ROTC unit in the nation, from among 272 programs.

ROTC, the well-known acronym for Reserve Officer Training Corps, is a command charged with preparing college students to become military officers. The various college programs are judged by a number of indicators, including how their cadets perform at summer camp, their grades, and how they progress through the ranks. Obviously, the folks at Central Missouri State are doing something right.

"We get great support from the university," Therese said. "We're seen as part of the team, so we have the luxury of choosing from the best. We look for scholars, athletes, and leaders. We attract young people who are active in church groups, community, or school activities, so they're already accustomed to team play—we build on that."

I was curious about the dynamic between the professional military staff and the cadets. Therese explained: "It's very much a cadet-run battalion. The cadets hold each other accountable; peer pressure and peer acceptance keep the team running smoothly. The egotistical types don't make it, even if they initially come across as leaders. The peer ratings favor team players over those who focus on themselves. The same is true for the cadre. I'm expected to know more than my department. Our defined lines are purposely kept fuzzy, so we all buy in to the overall mission."

Major Carmack served in Somalia in the early 1990s during Operation Restore Hope, a period I knew had been difficult for her. A lieutenant at the time, her forty-seven-person platoon provided petroleum support for the twenty-seven coalition countries. She was the only female officer in the compound.

"It was challenging," she told me. "I wasn't one of the guys in every sense of the word. There was always some distance out of respect. It was lonely and for awhile I was mad at the situation, the Army, and myself. My dad had died a few months before and I was away from my family, from whom I normally draw strength. Communication was difficult, the mail took fifteen days. For a while I wondered if I was in the right profession, but I think I'm a stronger person for the experience."

Did the experience provide any perspective for her role as a female officer in the ROTC battalion? Therese responded, "Most of our females are confident and strong-willed. 'Can-do' has replaced 'can't-do' and they compete well. While I'm not preoccupied with gender or race, I know from experience that isolation is stressful. We make sure cadets have a sponsor who understands their situation and can bridge any cultural gaps that might exist."

I asked about her newfound confidence and what she sees as the battalion's key to success. "Confidence is what you do with failure. I've bombed a bunch of stuff, but I've learned not to go into a shell over it. We tell our cadets—'It's not who you know, or what you know, it's what you do.' We're a bunch of doers. We make mistakes, but we go on."

It's a Tough Job, but Somebody's Got to Do It

The U.S. Military team has a hidden asset—the noncommissioned officer, or NCO for short.

The term *noncommissioned officer* is a misnomer. These guys aren't "non" anything—they do it all. I wish we had thought of a better term.

The military rank structure is a bit of an anachronism. We have commissioned officers—lieutenants, captains, majors, and the like—who are commissioned by the president with special authorities and responsibilities. Commissioned officers focus on strategy and the big decisions that must be made.

Commissioned officers execute through the NCO—what the Navy calls petty officers and the Army, Air Force, and Marines call sergeants.

If a military unit were an NFL football team, there'd be an NCO at quarterback and middle linebacker. If a lieutenant were coaching, then all his assistant coaches would be NCOs. The team's general manager, who sits up in a suite somewhere, would be a major, a colonel, or maybe a general. It's the general manager's job to oversee the whole operation—from establishing strategy, to procuring the best players, to selling tickets, to making sure the facilities are maintained. He's the guy responsible. He's a big-picture guy. He has a different educational background than the guys on the field. If he's smart, he has an NCO-like guy at his right hand to develop informal relationships with the players, pass messages, and be an extra set of eyes and ears. That person would be a sergeant major—a senior NCO.

Football won't work without quarterbacks, middle linebackers, and assistant coaches.

And it's the same way in the military. Our system won't work without NCOs.

NCOs come up through the ranks. Like football players, they've lived in the trenches and played through rain, snow, and sleet. They've been down in the mud and taken the hits. They joined as privates and got hooked on soldiering.

The average NCO makes about half what a commissioned officer makes.

It's a thankless task.

Who was Eisenhower's sergeant major? Or Schwartzkopf's?

You'll never hear their names or read their words, but I guarantee you they were doing a heck of a job.

There should be a national monument to the NCO.

Good NCOs are worth their weight in gold.

Good NCOs serve two masters—their officer and their men. It's a balancing act.

An NCO has the power to turn an officer into a hero or a villain. An officer is screwed with a counterproductive NCO. And many an officer has been made by the efforts of a great one.

NCOs are less political, less conflicted. They're more hands-on. When mistakenly referred to as "sir," they've been known to reply, "Don't call me 'sir,' I work for a living!"

There are some things an officer doesn't need to be involved with; that's why we have NCOs. As bad as it is, I'd rather see an officer doing NCO business than see an NCO who gets into officer business. Role acceptance is critical.

It's important that soldiers spend time with NCOs, so it's a big deal when an officer appears. That's why attention is called when an officer arrives on the scene. It's a distance thing with officers, and we want that distance calibrated for maximum effectiveness. NCOs help set the distance.

The greenest lieutenant technically outranks a sergeant major, so an officer with thirty seconds in service outranks an NCO with thirty years. On its face, it's nonsensical. But the beauty is that the sergeant major is going to help raise that lieutenant. The sergeant major will keep him straight. And any lieutenant who abuses his authority will not be long for the United States Military.

Like the petty officer told me at Fleet Training Center San Diego, "It's all team."

★ ★ ★   **STRATEGY 34**   ★ ★ ★

TAKE CARE OF YOUR LINE. Every team has linemen, guys who do the hard work down in the trenches. In the military we call these men and women noncommissioned officers, or NCOs for short. Our system won't work without NCOs. They're indispensable role players, who oversee the day-to-day running of a ship or unit and rarely see the glory that seems to be reserved for officers. Every team has this kind of people. Make sure they're taken care of; don't wait until they're gone to appreciate them.

The Army in Black and White

Northwestern University sociologist Charles Moskos is the coauthor of *All That We Can Be: Black Leadership and Racial Integration the Army Way*. His recent article for *Military Officer* magazine, "Overcoming Race: Army Lessons for Society," is good news for the Army team.

According to Moskos's survey data, black soldiers are three times more likely than black civilians to say race relations are better in the Army than in civilian life. Blacks make up about a quarter of the Army, including 25 percent of the junior enlisted force, 35 percent of noncommissioned officers, 12 percent of officers, and 8 percent of the general officer ranks. As Moskos points out, it's the only place in American society where whites are routinely supervised by blacks.

Race relations in the Army are far from perfect, but the Army is a textbook case of how the team dynamic can succeed—even where the population is predominantly young males, a group otherwise prone to trouble.

Key to the Army's success is its emphasis on team and the initiation process of boot camp, where core values are instilled. Rank, uniforms, and team effort tend to push racial issues into the background, especially when a unit is involved in challenging activities, with a common goal.

The Army maintains an uncompromising atmosphere of nondiscrimination. Evaluation reports for every officer, warrant officer, and sergeant require a brief analysis of whether the individual supports equal opportunity. A negative comment in this area ensures nonpromotion and a quick ticket to civilian life.

There is zero tolerance for racist behavior. Trained equal opportunity officers keep leaders apprised of the racial climate in their unit and investigate any incidents that occur.

Career success is based on performance, with defined standards. Moskos makes a good point here: Rather than lowering standards, the Army trains soldiers to meet standards that are uncompromising. The Army has one of the largest continuing education programs in the world. Some 60 percent of the participants in this program are black, forming a major training ground for black representation in the noncommissioned officer corps.

Further, the U.S. Military Academy Preparatory School functions as a thirteenth year of high school, preparing West Point candidates in academic competencies like reading, writing, and mathematics. It's an ideal program for candidates with a deficient high school background, and has helped increase diversity at West Point. Blacks who graduate from the prep school are just as likely to succeed at the academy as their white counterparts.

Ultimately, the test of diversity for the Army is whether or not it improves performance in a life-or-death industry. By enforcing standards, rooting out discrimination, focusing on mission, and emphasizing teamwork, the U.S. Army has ensured that the answer to that all-important question is yes.

★ ★ ★ **STRATEGY 35** ★ ★ ★

CROSS-TRAIN YOUR TEAM. Train as a team whenever possible. Team skills are different from individual skills. Get people out of their departments and into the big picture. This is how leaders are made and effective teams are built. Hire the best and train those who have the potential to be the best. Cross-train them to keep their comfort zone expanding, and your talent pool at maximum depth.

Teamwork—It Really Is Work

We sometimes think of teamwork as a mystical occurrence, because when we're a part of it, it feels like magic. The reality is that teamwork works best with a plan, some sacrifice of individual desires, constant communication, and a lot of work.

With a team, you leave the pleasant confines of just motivating yourself. The individuals around you will have different levels of commitment. You have to get them to buy in.

Buy-in is critical. When people don't buy in, they feel free to sit on the sidelines and criticize.

Clear those sidelines.

Put those people in the game.

Most of them will make it and become a part of the team. Others will take a few hits, decide it's not worth it, and cut themselves. Like I said, it's not easy.

Take the Navy approach, and train as a team whenever possible. There's a big difference between individual skills and team skills. Some things have to be learned as a team.

Stress communication. Don't let yourself be wandering on night patrol, where nobody knows the plan, the critical information, or how to get back safely. Communication makes clear what the desired results are, and to what standards team members will be held accountable. With accountability you get positive peer pressure to jump-start the nonperformers.

Get your people out of their departments and into the big picture. They won't want to go, but they need to. It's how leaders are made and effective teams are built. In the ROTC battalion at Central Missouri State, leaders were involved in all the activities of the battalion, not just their own little fiefdom. It's a big part of why they're number one in the nation.

Downplay elitism and stress the importance of role-playing. You need teammates willing to do the tough jobs without a lot of fanfare. In the military we call them noncommissioned officers. You need intermediate leaders who've been down in the trenches and understand what motivates the people who work for a living.

Resist the temptation to surround yourself with clones. A clone or two is fine, but when you've created a good-old-boy network you've gone too far. Hire people smarter than you. Go after the best, and train those who have potential to be the best.

Teamwork doesn't just happen. Like everything else worth building, it takes strategic design and relentless execution—otherwise known as work.

Train Tough Challenge

Make a list of the teams you're on. Don't forget family.

_____

_____

_____

Briefly critique each team's effectiveness.

_____

_____

_____

What one thing can you do to improve each team?

_____

_____

_____

12

——★——

LEADERSHIP

Something for Everyone

I've always had tremendous respect for the United States Marine Corps. The thing that always impressed me was how proud every marine I've ever met was about the organization.
—Coach Bobby "The General" Knight

I agree with Coach Knight on this one. I've served with a lot of marines and they never fail to impress—and surprise. The U.S. Marines are a mystery. How do they get the way they are? What's raises them to the next level? Who are these guys?

I grew up in awe of marines. I read about their battles with the Barbary pirates "on the shores of Tripoli," their epic World War II battles at Guadalcanal and Iwo Jima, and of course their surprise amphibious landing at Inchon during the Korean War. They'll go anywhere, always the first to fight. When America needs muscled involvement, "Send in the Marines!" is the call to action.

You would expect marines to be like professional wrestlers, full of bluster and hype. Who could blame them? They are clearly the baddest mamajamas in the valley. For the longest time I was very careful around marines, thinking the typical marine would find any excuse to pick a fight.

My experience has been just the opposite. Without exception, every marine with whom I've worked has been a perfect lady or gentleman.

Marine officers are the ultimate trip. They're the most mild-mannered people on earth. Some of them could be librarians. They're trained to kill you eleven different ways, and yet you feel like you're working with a missionary. It can be very unsettling.

Superman would have been a great marine—Clark Kent during day-to-day operations and Superman when push comes to shove. That's the way these guys operate. They're a unique breed.

Marines learn to lead by degrees. They master each level of leadership before they move on to the next, receiving positive reinforcement along the way. They model the leader ahead of them—who provides the example.

Marines believe that character is a choice, that values can be taught.

They actually teach tact, which they define as "the ability to deal with others without creating offense." They see tact as a leadership trait. It's a throwback to another era, but it works. Marines are some of the most polite people on earth.

Maybe that's why so many of them wind up as business CEOs. That mix of tact and the ability to thrive in an environment of stressful, continuous combat operations is pretty good preparation for the business world. Just add money.

If you see any of these guys out there, be sure and refer to them as "former Marines" not "ex-Marines." I'm not sure I understand the distinction, but they do. They're taught "once a marine, always a marine." It fits with their motto, *Semper Fidelis*—"Always Faithful."

★ ★ ★ **STRATEGY 36** ★ ★ ★

UNDERSTAND WHAT PEOPLE DON'T LIKE ABOUT THEIR LEADERS. People hate it when they don't understand where they stand with the boss. They don't like feeling threatened, or having their time wasted. They don't like bosses who are pedantic or hypocritical. If you can avoid these pitfalls, you're on your way to becoming an effective leader.

What Leaders Say About Their Leaders

This is not going to be scientific.

There are polls and surveys out there that will give you a valid statistical sampling and tell you a lot of the same things. But you won't get the passion.

Junior leaders get very passionate when they talk about their bosses. I know, I'm in the listening business. After a while, you get a pretty good idea of the things that turn on junior leaders, or drive them crazy.

Leadership can be an elusive concept to pin down. That's why it's the subject of countless studies and screeds. But if you can avoid the things that leaders hate about their leaders and build on the things that leaders love about their leaders, you'll be on your way to the band of excellence.

Here are the top five dislikes, in no particular order:

Enigmatic. We hate it when we don't understand the boss. We want to know where we stand, and what the rules are. We hate it when the leader is inconsistent, or plays head games. A common example is a leader who claims to value family time, yet gives his own family short shrift and rewards those who are obviously doing the same thing.

Threatening. We don't like the sword of Damocles over our head. We don't like to see coworkers in that position either. Scapegoating, the act of torturing a subordinate for the sins of all, is a big no-no. It's entertaining to a point, but no one wants to be the next in line for humiliation. We expect our leaders to be able to discipline their passions and keep control of their emotions.

Hypocritical. If you're an evil person, please let us know. We'll be able to tell soon enough if you're self-serving. But please don't say one thing and do another. It's very confusing and gives virtue a bad name.

Pedantic. Attention to detail is one thing, but let us do our jobs. When you're down in the hold rearranging the baggage, it makes us very nervous about who's steering the ship.

Wasting our time. We understand the need for meetings. Hey, you're the boss. But we have a job to do here. Can we please get some respect for our time? Can we start on time? Can there please be some semblance of organization to the time we spend together? Jeez.

OK, we've been pretty hard on you. But we're equally passionate about the things we like in our leaders. Here they are:

Courage. We love it when you take risks. We'll feed off your confidence, and make you a legend. But we also want to see that "three o'clock in the morning courage," the courage to keep fighting when the whole thing seems to be coming down around our ears. We love fighters.

★ ★ ★   **STRATEGY 37**   ★ ★ ★

UNDERSTAND WHAT PEOPLE ADMIRE IN THEIR LEADERS. People want
to see courage, the courage to keep fighting when the whole thing
seems to be coming down around your ears. Let people know where
the goal line is. Make yourself a temporary equal once in a while and
really, really listen. Be fair—that's harder than it seems at first blush.
At the end of the day, people want your trust. If you can't give it right
away, at least let people earn it.

Openness. Let's communicate. We can tell whether you want the real
answers to your questions, or you're just showing off. How much
noise can you handle? Because the clash of ideas is noisy. Challenging the prevailing wisdom always is. Openness means making
yourself a temporary equal once in a while and listening for the information that only the lower ranks can give you.

Drive to win. Sure, we all have different levels of commitment, but, at
heart, we all want to be winners. Set clear goals for us. We'll block,
carry the ball, or whatever, but we want to know what the goal is. The
ten? The three? A touchdown? We'll fight awfully hard for those last
few yards if we know where the goal line is. We want to see you committed to victory, however you define it.

Fairness. We know life is tough. Not everybody is going to make it. But
we want to feel like we all have an equal chance to succeed. Mentorship is one thing; cronyism is another. Just be fair.

Trust. At the end of the day we want your trust. If you give us the benefit of the doubt, we'll live up to your highest expectations. The
greatest gift you can give us is your trust. If you can't give it, at least
let us earn it. Trust is more effective than keeping us on edge all the
time, and it makes for a much better environment. Even building
trust is OK.

Everyone's a Leader

The premise that everyone's a leader is central to our thinking in the
United States Military. It's part of who we are. We cultivate leaders like a

farmer cultivates a field. Of course, some pumpkins grow bigger than others.

One of the beauties of our hierarchical system is that every leader is a follower. No matter how far you advance, you've always got a boss. And it's part of the boss's job to grow you to the next level.

Role modeling is key. As junior leaders, we learn to sift through the leadership characteristics of those up the line, inculcating what works and discarding what doesn't.

But the absolute rock-bottom issue for leaders is commitment.

Are you willing to step into leadership?

That's not good enough.

You have to dive in.

Leadership is a full-time job. Sitting on the side of the pool with your feet in the water will not get it done.

Splashing around will not get it done.

Leadership is first and foremost commitment. It's involvement.

That's why the first challenge of leadership is always internal.

When I swim as part of my conditioning program, I arrive at the pool with a predetermined number of laps that I will swim. I don't hit the pool and say to myself, "Gee, I don't feel so great. Maybe I'll just float around and go home."

I'm committed to my laps.

It's always a shock hitting the water; in fact, it's one the worst feelings I can think of. Unless I think about the challenges of leadership, many of which feel even worse.

Leadership is tough. Good leadership is even tougher.

There's nothing worse than being in a leadership position you're trying to avoid. Avoidance behaviors are far worse than the pains of acceptance. You spend a lot of time and energy looking for shortcuts, and you feel lousy for it.

Might as well dive in. Sure, there's some unpleasantness, but the rewards are tremendous.

Leadership is commitment. You can cover a multitude of sins if at heart you're committed. Commitment will see you through.

Of course there are a few admonitions you might find helpful, once you're committed.

Learn to Like People. There's a common misconception about the military: that all our leaders have to do is give orders and the troops fall in line.

We do fall in line when so ordered, but that's about as far as it goes. Otherwise, we're just like everybody else. We want to know why and who said.

The few times in my career when I lost patience and settled issues by giving orders were memorable—and counterproductive. "Because I said so" brings back unhappy memories for a lot of people. You never get the response you want when you use those words.

Leadership is about consensus building. It's hard. It takes energy, and sometimes people are unreasonable. The guy who said, "Hell is other people," wasn't far off.

But you gotta love 'em. You've got to care. You've got to put the needs of your team ahead of yourself.

Share power.

As a leader, you're in the enabling business. You generate power and empower.

You're in the business of taking disparate people and turning them into like-minded people—not in the sense that they all think alike, but that they share common goals and values.

Making this happen will test your interpersonal competence.

It helps if you develop a love for people. It helps if you care.

Take the High Road. It's your job as a leader to make decisions at the forks in the road. The troops are going to follow.

Nowhere is this more true than in your ethical decision making.

Get it through your head that leadership entails ethical visibility, that your ethics are on display. Your ethical example represents the organization.

When we promote soldiers to sergeant, we move them to another section or unit. We want them to have a fresh start as leaders, without any immature indiscretions as part of their baggage.

Soldiers who succeed in Officer Candidate School are moved to a new location when they are commissioned as officers. They get as fresh a start as we can give them, because the ethical demands on leaders are so much greater.

As a leader, you shape culture. You'll get the kind of behavior you demonstrate—or tolerate.

Commit to the high road.

Inspire. You're in the inspiration business.

Think of it this way: If you can inspire someone to take action, it's one less job you have to do yourself, or hire someone else to do.

Inspiration yields high dividends. Plus, it's one of the really fun parts of being a leader.

Lead from the front whenever possible. People want to look up to their leaders, and they admire courage.

Let me give you two examples.

In boot camp the cadre had us lined up, ready to climb up and over a huge ladder with rungs that were set farther apart as the height increased. A demonstrator showed us how to climb it, carefully negotiating each rung. Then our company commander arrived in his jeep, peeled off his shirt, and catapulted himself from rung to rung, going up and over in mere seconds. We went nuts. We had a new hero.

Later in my career, while assigned to an intelligence unit, we were taken to a range to fire captured Soviet weaponry. Our brigade commander fired every weapon first, dead on target. He took out a tank with a Soviet rocket-propelled grenade—first try. It was impressive. He was a guy who took the lead, who wasn't afraid of failure. We fed off that for a long time.

You don't have to climb ladders or blow up tanks. But get out of that "above the fray" mentality, and show your people what you're made of.

Think. It's your mind that uniquely qualifies you for the position of leadership in which you find yourself. It's why you're in the nuclear power business instead of the shoe business, or vice versa.

Your particular kind of thinking and your ability to access experience are what uniquely qualify you for the job. You've got the systems understanding, the ability to see crises in advance and plan for contingencies.

It's your obligation to think. To find vision. To strategize. People are following you. You're the leader.

★ ★ ★ STRATEGY 38 ★ ★ ★

DIVE INTO LEADERSHIP. The first challenge of leadership is internal. There's no halfway—leadership is a full-time job. As a leader you shape culture, so always take the high road. You're in the inspiration business, so look for opportunities to show your people what you're made of. Learn to like people. Think. It's your mind that uniquely qualifies you for the position of leadership in which you find yourself. It's your obligation to think, strategize, and find the vision.

Leadership Versus Management

Gather a group of military officers for a discussion on leadership and you inevitably get into the leadership versus management debate. In an organization where "everyone's a leader," we still do a lot of managing. So it's an interesting discussion.

Inevitably we agree that leaders still grapple with management functions, and managers still need leadership skills.

Management focuses on planning, organizing, budgeting, and accounting; leadership on visioning, motivating, modeling, and directing.

Fortunately, we have a near perfect role combination spread throughout our military: commanders and executive officers (XOs). The commander focuses on leadership and the XO on management. It's a team sport. They work hand in glove to be successful, with the commander focusing on the big picture and the XO coordinating the details.

The commander liaises with higher headquarters and inspires the troops. The executive officer oversees the work of the staff, translating the commander's vision into concrete action.

The commander is chief communicator; the XO is his number one translator.

The commander asks a lot of questions; the XO runs around finding answers.

A good executive officer frees the commander to look outside the unit for fresh ideas.

A good commander stays out of the weeds, trusting the XO to run the day-to-day business of the unit.

It's a good system, and it works.

What Leaders Dare Not Delegate

The fine art of delegation is central to successful leadership. Leaders who try to do too much find themselves bogged down in a mire of endless detail.

Many times the same attribute that got a leader in a leadership position in the first place is the same attribute that will lead to leadership failure: the ability to get things done. The personal ability to solve problems is a nice skill to have, unless it gets in the way of leadership. Leaders should rarely be problem solvers. Problem solving is time and energy intensive and will quickly push leadership priorities out of the way.

For someone who's an adept problem solver, letting go is difficult. There's an adrenalin rush to the frenzy of problem solving, an almost Zen-like experience in the midst of detail. It's addictive.

The challenge is even greater for perfectionists, who come to feel every action should be accomplished "just so." The rule of thumb for delegation is that if a subordinate can accomplish the mission to 75 percent of your personal best effort, delegate it. It's more important that you focus on your leadership role.

But there are some things leaders should not delegate—such as the people part of business.

As a leader, you've got to stay involved in the careers of your people—from the hiring process, to performance evaluations, to bonuses and promotions. I spent a good part of my career in human resources, and the best commanders I saw were the ones giving people plenty of face time. They were involved in finding the best people, developing them, and seeing that they were taken care of. You can't lead without the led.

Leaders are also the primary time managers for the operation. Not only do they set the tone for valuing time, but they need to be consciously involved in time management decisions. Leaders should ask themselves, "How can I squeeze the most out of my people's time, without wearing them out?"

Think of it as looking for quality minutes. A few here and a few there can really add up. Wasted days and wasted nights can kill you.

In military units there's always an issue about when to conduct physical training, or PT. Morning is clearly the best time from a training standpoint, but then you have to give the troops cleanup time and time to grab breakfast. By the time you get them back it's 9:00 A.M. Some of them are invigorated, but a lot of them are worn out, too—and the day is just starting.

When I took command of a unit during the Desert Storm buildup, the first thing I did was move PT to the afternoon. My troops were under tremendous pressure to perform and I wanted them focused on their jobs first thing in the morning. We had work call at 7:30 A.M. and broke for PT at 4:00 P.M. The troops were free to call it a day immediately after PT, so they were cleaning up and getting dinner on their own time—and we were eking an extra half hour of work from every soldier in the unit. Importantly, we were also getting more morning time. Hey, we were getting ready for a war.

Good leaders are good time managers. They're cognizant of their people's time. Meetings are organized and productive, not mindless endurance exercises. Good leaders show their involvement in people's time at every opportunity and work to permeate their philosophy throughout the organization.

Leaders must also know when a project demands their personal attention. There are some things that are so important you have to throw delegation out the window and get personally involved.

I had one such moment after assuming duties as Adjutant General for the Combined Arms Center and Fort Leavenworth, Kansas. The garrison was commanded by Colonel William L. Hart, or "Big Bill," as we sometimes referred to him. Hart was a football player, and a perfectly proportioned 6'7", 250 pounds. One of the last guys out of Vietnam, he had also served as warden of the U.S. Disciplinary Barracks, the military's maximum security prison. He was a guy who got your attention.

"Mark," he told me, "you'll have wide latitude in this job, I won't be in your knickers. Just make sure in-processing runs smoothly, it's the one thing you don't want to screw up. It'll set the tone for everything you do here."

By in-processing I knew he meant the 1,000 majors who would arrive in a couple weeks to attend the Command and General Staff College. My people had already assured me they had things well in hand.

But Hart wasn't buying it. "When you're the leader," he told me, "sometimes you're the only one who's right."

I decided to get personally involved.

On the surface, everything was fine. In-processing was an annual affair and worked OK from a bureaucrat's perspective. But as I checked under the rocks it became apparent that in-processing was a far cry from what it should be.

The plan called for the majors to be filling out forms that repeatedly asked for the same information. Worse, they'd be standing in line after line in the college hallways. In-processing for the college had become notorious, with students showing up hours early and sitting in lawn chairs to beat the crowd. Everyone else could look forward to standing in the halls. It was no way to run a railroad for privates, much less for field grade officers.

It was too late to redesign the entire process, but I was determined to have an impact.

"What's the long pole in the tent?" I asked the team. "Who takes the most time with each individual?"

DELEGATE, BUT KNOW WHAT NOT TO DELEGATE. You won't get far without the ability to delegate. The ability to solve problems is a nice skill to have, unless it gets in the way of leadership. Some things you can delegate; others you must hang onto. Don't delegate the people part of business. Stay involved in hiring, firing, evaluation, bonuses, and promotions. You can't lead without the led. Leaders are also the primary time managers for the operation. Good leaders show their involvement in people's time at every opportunity, and work to permeate their philosophy throughout the organization.

"Finance" was the unanimous response.

As it turned out, most of the rest of the process kept a steady pace. By focusing on finance we were able to break down their part of the system and streamline it.

But I was still hearing echoes of "we've always done it this way."

In-processing always started at 9:00 A.M. sharp. By that time a long line of unhappy majors would build up. The only thing preventing a riot was the general goodwill of the newly arrived and the hope that bumping into some old pals would keep them occupied.

"Start at eight," I directed, after listening to all the arguments. "We won't change the advertised start time, but let's reward the early birds, do away with the line, and get some practice perfecting our system before they arrive in big numbers."

This wasn't rocket science. It was harder. I was breaking through the bureaucratic mind-set, in a situation where delegation was not going to get it done.

As we went along that morning, we found that the classrooms made excellent waiting areas for the occasional overflow. We turned on the TVs and made it as comfortable as we could. It had to beat standing in line.

I was privileged to serve through two more in-processings and was less involved in each one. My subordinates got it, becoming creative at a level of detail that would never have occurred to me. In-processing became a project I could delegate, as we leveraged technology to streamline the effort—and radically reduced the inconvenience to our customers, the majors.

Because it occurred in the first month of the job, the in-processing effort set the tone for my time as Adjutant General. Getting into the detail of the operation allowed me to integrate my key themes with some otherwise mundane activities. The message was clear: Challenge the status quo, find a better way, and take care of people.

I also went on to enjoy serving under the leadership of Colonel Hart. When he asked me what time it was, he wasn't asking how my watch worked. We developed a coded communication that served us well throughout the remainder of our military careers and into civilian life, where we are business partners.

A Matter of Style

One of the challenges in encouraging people to step up to leadership is the mistaken belief that without a certain personality and style, you're not cut out to lead. The image of George S. Patton comes to mind. But Patton ought to be a source of encouragement—he studied leadership his entire career, and learned to tweak his personality and style to fit the situation. Patton worked at leadership, and demonstrated that the effort pays off.

Leaders adapt to situations, and employ different techniques as the situation warrants. As a brand-new second lieutenant, I was beholden to my senior sergeants for expertise and experience. My style was very supporting, involving them early on in decisions.

Later, I assumed more of a coaching style, one that I was comfortable with from my athletic training. Occasionally, as performance demands grew and time was at a premium, my style took on a more confident, directive nature. Finally, as I moved up in the hierarchy and assumed a wider responsibility, the art of delegation became key.

My leadership range increased as I gained experience and moved from positions of daily, direct contact with subordinates to situations where my troops were spread over a wide geographic range and contact was often indirect.

Vastly different leadership styles can still be effective.

The First Infantry Division, "The Big Red One," as we are proud to call it, offers an interesting case in point. While serving with the division, I heard about the notorious change of command between General Terry Allen and General Clarence Huebner in the summer of 1943. It's still a topic for discussion sixty years later.

General Allen was a personable, inspirational leader who led the division through North Africa and a difficult landing in Sicily. Still, General

Omar Bradley made the decision to replace General Allen. He felt the division had become overconfident and might not be adequately prepared for the much tougher fighting to come.

It was not a popular decision, especially when the far less personable Huebner was named as Allen's replacement.

Huebner was a no-nonsense disciplinarian whose emphasis was fundamentals—not a popular subject for a battle-hardened unit. His pet rock was marksmanship; he expected soldiers to be experts with their personal weapons.

When Huebner saw weaknesses he expected them to be corrected, knowing that such adjustments would save lives down the line. While he faced considerable internal opposition, his standards never wavered.

He immersed himself in the details of combat, personally mastering weaponry and demonstrating personal courage to his troops by allowing a tank to roll over him as he crouched in a foxhole. Further, Huebner knew how to take care of soldiers, ensuring they were rested, well fed, and had the equipment they needed.

Huebner would never be as beloved as General Allen, but his high training standards and attention to detail paid big dividends. "The Big Red One" hit the beach at Normandy and effectively carried the fight into Germany. Using a different leadership style, Huebner took the division to another level.

Leadership makes a difference.

Effective leaders get the most of people; great leaders inspire them.

Leaders perform with the added responsibility of setting the moral tone for their operations, and nothing, absolutely nothing, relieves them of the responsibility to fix the course, set standards—and think.

Train Tough Challenge

As you look back over this chapter, what do you see as your biggest strength as a leader? Biggest weakness?

Strength

_____

Weakness

_____

Think about how you can maximize your biggest strength as a leader, and identify ways to shore up your biggest weakness.

_____

_____

_____

_____

_____

PART FOUR

— ★ —

YOUR PERSONAL
BATTLE PLAN

Life is a battle. You need allies.
You need a plan.

13

——— ★ ———

TACTICS

Going for the Win

Activities at the tactical level of war focus on the application of combat power to defeat an enemy at a particular time and place. Tactics can be thought of as the art and science of winning engagements and battles.
—Warfighting Manual of the United States Marines

This is the most important chapter in the book. This is the chapter you read if you could read only one. Because this is the chapter that picks up where the manual leaves off. This is the stuff they tell you in the officers' club after a beer. The unwritten stuff.

A career in the United States Military is extremely fast-paced. You're always moving from assignment to assignment, and you're always changing bosses. You see the world and the good, the bad, and the ugly side of a lot of leaders.

In a twenty-year career you'll probably serve in ten different locations and have thirty different bosses. You learn how to adapt quickly, or you're lost. You learn how to play the game, or you're gone. You learn fast because you're in a fast-paced environment. You see a lot in a relatively short period of time.

The higher you go, the tougher it gets. The only ones left are the winners.

My military career was totally unique. I was a soldier jock. I make no claims to being a great athlete, other than that I was always out there busting my hump for the win. Because I had only moderate physical gifts, I had to find the angles in order to be successful. I worked hard to master the strategy and tactics of each particular sport.

What I found was that a lot of the principles I was employing on the sports field were similar to what I was learning in the military. Planning. Training. Leadership. Teamwork. Strategy and tactics.

And now I'm going to show you how to apply them to your life.

A military career is tough. There were times when I was knocked flat on the canvas. The only thing that got me back up was the theme from *Rocky* and the deep-down belief that if I could block a few punches and get to swinging again I would be all right. Like I say, there's a lot of similarity between sports and the military. A sound strategy and a tactical mind-set are critical to success.

This chapter is about how that process works.

Remember the discussion in Chapter 5 on endstate? The business of understanding the mission? That was a very important chapter, because before you can go for the win you've got to define what a win is.

It's different for everybody. But it's important for every person to have an endstate vision—a state of being toward which you are striving. The vision includes health, wealth, career, and personal goals. Strategy outlines how you're going to go about achieving your goals; tactics addresses the finite details of implementing that strategy. Tactics are always subordinate to strategy, just as strategy is subordinate to the vision.

For the purposes of this chapter I'm going to assume you're going all out for the win, that you're in a be-all-you-can-be mode. Type A all the way. You want to be the type of person that people approach and say, "We're impressed. We'd like you to run for president. Please come and run our country."

Now I realize not everybody is like that. But once in a while it's important to think that way. You can always tone it down later.

How would you run your life if you thought you were presidential material?

Keeping in mind your moral and ethical boundaries, ask yourself: "What are the tactics that lead to the win?"

That's what this chapter is about.

Think of life as a board game, with its unique strategy, tactics, and rules. You've probably played a board game, only to find out as you went along that the rules were different than you thought they were. You have to get zapped a few times before you figure out what's going on.

That's the way life is. "If I'd only known then what I know now" is a common refrain.

The key is to learn faster, quickly mastering the tactics and techniques that lead to victory.

"I don't play games," you might be saying. "Game playing is superficial."

That's fine. Delude yourself. Whether you admit it or not, you'll be playing—just not as well.

Because the gamers will be playing hardball.

Yes, this chapter will be superficial. *Deeply* superficial.

We've laid the groundwork, in depth, in the preceding chapters. Now it's time to go out to the training area for some force-on-force training.

We're going to school on career tactics and the bending of bureaucracy by force of will.

★ ★ ★ **STRATEGY 40** ★ ★ ★

DO THE EASY STUFF. Timeliness. Courtesy. Personal appearance. The nuances of career advancement can be quite complex, yet it's amazing how many people overlook the basics. Don't make a tough job tougher by missing the career discriminators that can make a difference. Be a problem solver. Be the best at something. Stay on top of the technological developments in your field. And for heaven's sake, do the easy stuff.

Career Material

Everybody has a career, though it may not seem like much of one. That's OK. Life is a full-time job. It's all in how you look at it.

Even entrepreneurs have careers, though they operate in a different mode than most of the rest of us. They don't normally have bosses, but they do have customers and people they want to partner with. Entrepreneurs also have good imaginations, and since they're often somebody else's boss, they can reverse some of what I'm saying and still make money with it.

Let's get one other thing straight right from the beginning: Everything I say here depends on one attribute—competence. The tactics I discuss here will help you hide ignorance for a while, but to really maximize their effect you have to learn your job. Otherwise, you just get good at covering up.

It's like I tell athletes who are trying out for a ball team: There are a number of things you can do to maximize your chances for making the team, but ultimately, you have to be able to field ground balls.

So the first question is: Have I mastered all the nuances that come with my career?

Not many can answer that question in the affirmative.

The second question is: Why not?

The answer to the second question opens a Pandora's box of issues. If the answer is "it's boring" or "it's too complicated," then you're probably in the wrong career field. It's hard to learn something you're not interested in.

But let's close Pandora's box for right now and drive on. I want to cover career material in four pieces.

Moron Competence. Originally I wanted to call this section "More on Competence," but the more I thought about it, "Moron Competence" seemed apropos. Competence is the skill set you need to perform your particular function; moron competence is the complementary skill set of which most people are unaware. You need both to be successful.

The first rule of moron competence is to do the easy stuff. It's amazing how many people fail in the simplest part of their job—what I call the easy stuff.

As an Army officer my job could be extremely complex. Some of it taxed every bit of my will and desire. Some of it was really, really hard.

But when I looked at an Army officer's report card, I found most of the hard stuff was graded in a subjective manner. After all the work was done, it was hard to tell who had done the best job.

The only totally objective item on the report card was the physical training test score.

Very few Army officers attain the maximum score, but I found that with a little effort on my push-ups, sit-ups, and two-mile run, I could max the test every time.

I'm sure some of my report cards looked the same as a lot of other guys' cards, except mine always had a max test score. I figured, all things being equal, I would give a promotion board at least one good reason to promote me. I can hear the board now, "You know, this guy is a bit of a moron, but at least he's in good shape."

So do the easy stuff. Don't make a tough job tougher by overlooking the career discriminators that can make a difference. Timeliness. Courtesy. Personal appearance. Enthusiasm.

Remember when the teacher used to give five points for neatness? Take the points.

Here's another tip: Assume you can figure things out.

Be a problem solver.

Drop "I have no idea," from your response list. Don't expect every answer to be a slam dunk. Expect to have to grapple. Always have an idea. Do something in the direction of solving the problem, and you're on your way.

Master the language of your career field. Build a professional vocabulary. Understand the data—even if you don't trust it. If you don't trust the data, know why.

Stay involved with the technological developments in your field. Use the software and systems your people are using, so you know how they're doing things and what their challenges are.

Be the best at something. Showcase your talents, odd though they may be.

At the end of the Cold War I was in an infantry unit in Germany. Our German partner unit was an armor outfit. They invited us to spend a day with them to show us how they did business. Also on the agenda was a friendly volleyball match.

Right away I smelled a rat.

I knew the Germans pretty well by that time, and I knew as a group they were going to be good volleyball players. They were bringing us over for some schooling.

Not on my watch.

It so happens that I'm a very good volleyball player. Further, I do not like to be shown up.

Now my boss was a total spastic. This guy knew how to kill Russians twelve different ways, but he knew nothing about sports. I asked him to let me organize the team.

We beat those Germans like George Patton. We were nice about it, and later we drank their delicious beer and extolled the genius of Erwin Rommel. It all worked out.

Afterward the boss pulled me over and said, "Nice job." That's boss talk for "Without you we would surely have been humiliated."

And that brings me to my next subject. . . .

Boss Management. The first rule of boss management is to love the boss. Just as you should love the people who work under you, you've got to love the boss. A lot of people have a problem with that. But let's face it, this person is going to be a major player in your career. So get positive.

I loved 90 percent of the bosses I had in the military. Out of the thirty-plus bosses I had, there were only two or three I couldn't accommodate.

Bad bosses happen. But if you're going through boss after boss with problems, the problem is with you. The best thing to do with a really bad boss is to get out from under. But that should be the case only 10 percent of the time.

The rest of the time you should be looking for things to like about the boss. If he's not involved, that gives you latitude. If he's a bit of a dunderhead, that makes you the smart one. If he's driven, that means you're along for the ride.

Find things to like about the boss. Let him feel the love. Show some respect. Adopt a wee bit of humility. Think of it this way: If you're so smart, how come he's the boss? The two of you are in this thing together. Generally, you're thinking a lot more about him than he is about you. So you have the opportunity to make it a positive relationship, but you've got to manage the situation.

Understand your exact distance from the boss and the advantages and disadvantages of where you are. Late in my career I had an office right across the hall from the boss. After every cup of coffee he barged in with a new, great idea. He was killing me.

In my next job the boss was 200 miles away. I got a little lazy and sloppy from the lack of stimulation. These situations require adjustment.

In the first instance I eventually realized that of the twenty or so officers that the boss supervised, I had the inside track. I was closest to him and, despite the constant distractions, I always had his ear and I always knew what was going on. I came to see it as an advantage.

In the second instance I eventually woke up and realized that distance gave me the freedom to be my own man and run things my way, without the constant interference. I just had to work harder to keep the boss informed.

One of the greatest fallacies ever perpetrated on the senior/subordinate relationship is the "yes-man fallacy." It was started by jealous naysayers who watched the yes-men getting promoted ahead of them.

Now we have leaders all spewing the same lingo: "I don't want yes-men."

What a crock.

Regardless of what they say, leaders crave affirmation. More important, they're looking for people they can task. They're looking to delegate. The last thing they want to hear is "no," or in so many words, "I can't do it because . . ."

Rarely, if ever, should you say no up front, to the boss—even if it's a dumb idea and not your job.

Just say yes, even when it hurts.

You can always say no later—after you've done some work, set up the counterattack, and the boss is less emotionally invested in her great new idea.

If the boss wants your opinion, she'll ask for it. But when bosses are passing out taskings, they're looking for yes-men. Give her "three bags full, ma'am." And straighten her out later if you have to.

I learned a very important lesson in the first job of my career: Follow the leader, not the led.

There I was, a new second lieutenant with a full colonel telling me he wanted Fort Ord, California, to be the first post in the entire U.S. Military to have the Post Exchange System take over the management of our movie theaters.

All the bureaucrats said it couldn't be done.

The captains and majors said it would never happen.

Even his deputy, a lieutenant colonel, said it was a dumb idea.

So I went back to the colonel and told him all I'd heard.

Wrong answer.

It was going to happen. It did happen. Fort Ord was first, and the entire military soon followed.

Turns out the colonel knew more than the bureaucrats. He saw the playing field from a different perspective—from the top.

He then performed for me what we call in the military a "head space and timing adjustment"—a personal adaptation of a procedure normally reserved for a .50-caliber machine gun. I left his office a changed man. I had been to the mountain.

From that day forward I concentrated on following the leader, not the led.

Get up for Special Events. Special events are your chance to shine. From the company sales conference to the company golf tournament, special events allow you to showcase talents that might otherwise remain hidden. Make sure you're hitting all cylinders for these events.

Start with your approach to meetings, especially those the boss chairs. These aren't just meetings, they're events. The company pecking order is very often established by who does well in this setting. Bring something to the banquet, even if it's a ham sandwich.

If someone is briefing stats that reflect on your department, make sure you know what they are. Get to these meetings early, so you can find out whether the truth has changed since you last saw the reports—it often does.

You don't want to find yourself saying, "I don't know why my copier costs are ten times higher than everybody else's. Possibly because I'm an uninvolved manager who enjoys squandering the company's resources. Please kill me now."

There's usually a perfectly beautiful explanation—something like, "Those costs include the legal department; actually, they're down 50 percent from last year, and our new system will cut them in half again next year."

The point is, you're more likely to have a good response if you know what's coming.

Meetings where you stand up and present your own material offer another challenge. In general, "be brief, be brilliant, and be gone," is the best advice. But it's all relative. You have to gauge your approach to what the other people are doing and find your own niche. Usually less material, presented well, is the best option.

The same goes for those round-the-table, show-and-tell meetings with the boss. This setting is not the time for introducing inscrutable problems or airing dirty laundry with your peers. Bring something—normally one to three items—and keep them simple and positive. Thank people publicly at this kind of meeting. Once in a while just say "pass" when it's your turn, and then glance to the next brainiac, signaling that the floor is his or hers. Everyone will love the gift of time with which you have endowed them. The likelihood that the boss will remember some horrible thing for you to address actually decreases with the amount of time you have the floor.

Never underestimate inspections. Inspections go by numerous names now, invented to mask their true intent—euphemisms like "visits," "assistance," and "surveys." Most of the "assistance" I received on these occasions I really didn't need.

Do not allow underlings to set the tone for these blessed events. They sometimes have a vested interest in downplaying anything that involves work.

Don't be lulled into complacency. If anything, create a sense of panic. Check everything. Make it a big deal. It's a golden opportunity to generate energy and fix a few things before somebody comes in and fixes them for you. Inspections can actually make your job as a leader easier.

Have a Plan. Every career should have a plan. Plot your own advancement. Know where you want to go next. Seek responsibility. Take the tough jobs.

But always look before you leap. Ask around.

Know when to abandon ship. Every naval vessel has a practiced plan for this worst-case scenario. You should have one too. There's a yin and yang to every company, department, and industry. Timing is important. There's a sixth sense involved, but you can learn a lot by studying history and watching the trends.

I learned a lot while writing and researching *Trial By Basketball: The Life and Times of Tex Winter.*

Tex is a basketball coach, very much a genius in his field. His coaching career spans more than half a century. For the longest time he took coaching jobs where the deck was stacked against him. He did well, often with marginal talent. But he also coached through some very tough years.

In the end, he wound up coaching Michael Jordan longer than any other coach. He racked up six NBA championship rings on the coaching staff of the Chicago Bulls. Then he left for the Los Angeles Lakers, with Kobe Bryant and Shaquille O'Neal, and racked up three more.

What Tex will tell you is that it's a lot more fun working with the best. He'll go on to say that winning covers a multitude of sins. There are a lot of advantages to going with the best.

So hire the best people you can get, or move to where they are.

And have a plan.

★ ★ ★ **STRATEGY 41** ★ ★ ★

PLAN YOUR CAREER. Seek responsibility. Take the tough jobs, the ones that will stretch you and show what you can do. Master the basics of managing your boss. Get up for special events—opportunities where you can shine. Dominate the meeting game, and never, ever underestimate inspections—even when they're called "assistance visits" or "surveys." Set the tone for these blessed events.

The Battle of Bureaucratic Hill

I look at it this way: Bureaucracy is all around us, it's in every organization with which we deal, and it's part of the organizations we lead and manage. We've also internalized it, so it's also a part of who we are.

It's a significant part of the game of life. A part of life most of us find extremely frustrating.

I use the term *bureaucracy* in the large sense, as a code word for the overall process of interfacing with society for the purpose of getting things done. So by my definition, the moment you ask someone to do something, you're up against bureaucracy. When you seek to right a wrong, it's staring you in the face.

Your effectiveness as a human being is tested by how well you play bureaucracy, or it plays you. I was a pretty good player in my day and, believe me, the U.S. Military is a bureaucracy that plays for keeps. So I'm giving you the benefit of my years of experience in the big leagues.

The first thing to understand is that you are completely surrounded by incompetence. The competence that does exist we can be genuinely thankful for; it's what holds the center together. But if you're alive at all you're painfully aware of how wrong things can go, and how hard it is to make them right again.

I could list the foul-ups from this week alone. But I won't. It's constant. You undoubtedly have your own list of broken promises, dead-end answers, and unreturned phone calls and e-mails. It's insidious, and it only seems to get worse.

The increase in legal considerations slows play across the board. Personnel cuts make it harder and harder to link with a human problem solver, and the dumbing down of our educational system means that the humans we do link with will be only marginally competent.

Technology is in the plus column, but only for those who can use it to advantage.

As they say, it's tough out there.

Playing bureaucracy is one of the toughest games in town. Like a good general, you have to pick your battles. Wading into the fray only makes martyrs. Pick and choose, and learn to accept that the small stuff is not always going to go your way.

But you can fight city hall. You'll need a strategy, sound tactics, and the motivation to see the battle through. Bureaucracies depend on wearing out opponents, and often exhibit bullylike behavior. But like bullies everywhere they don't always stand up to confrontation; even the threat of counterattack can send them reeling. It takes that special combination of art and science.

Here are three tactics for conquering bureaucracy:

1. **Take notes.** Bureaucracies thrive on your lack of attention. Write down whom you spoke to, when you spoke to them, and what was said. You'll forget fast, so write it down and keep a file. They'll forget even faster, and they'll be very impressed when you can cite specifics in your next call. Bureaucrats freak when they think you're taking notes.

2. **Create a crisis.** "A failure to plan on your part does not constitute a crisis on mine" is a bureaucrat's favorite saying, but it's not true. Use judgment with this one, but understand that the hot cases go to the front of the line. If you're in a crisis situation, make sure you convey urgency and turn up the heat. If you can get them in crisis mode, they become very accommodating.

3. **Go to the top.** When it's just you against the machine, you still have the ultimate power of escalation. Nothing drains the blood from a bureaucrat's head faster than the merest hint that you'll take things up the hierarchy. Escalation presents a whole host of unpleasant possibilities for bureaucrats: explanations, questions about their people skills, and the professional embarrassment of having someone up the line overrule their intransigence. Regardless how cool the response to this suggestion, believe me, it has the same general effect of swatting the guy with a two-by-four. Now who's got the power? Mr. Won't-Say-Yes?

Those of us who work for a living face the everyday challenge of working in bureaucracy. Still, there's hope. Here are three tactics for thriving in bureaucracies:

1. **Strike while the iron is hot.** Bureaucracies have their own rhythms, and the wise manager uses these rhythms to advantage. Prior to Desert Storm the U.S. Military grappled with the prospect of downsizing our presence in Europe. It was a daunting task, com-

plete with naysayers and bureaucratic wrangling. Desert Storm necessitated that we send thousands of these troops to the Middle East, where they performed remarkably. Rather than reacclimating them to Germany, we touched them down and immediately began the process of getting them home. Heck, they'd just won a war; the business of moving back to the States was a piece of cake. Timing is everything.

2. **Find out who controls the money.** In every organization there are official and unofficial ways of doing business. Master both, but find out who controls the money and cultivate a relationship with this person. Sure, there are boards and processes, most of which take time and effort. Then there's someone who understands these processes—who knows how to shortcut red tape when the situation warrants. Find this person, and get acquainted.

3. **Protect your assets.** Hire the best people you can, train them well, and protect them. Learn the internal politics of downsizing, right-sizing, and reorganization. Keep your ear to the ground, and stay connected to the power brokers. Life is not fair in this arena. Like a rebounder in basketball, be prepared to use your elbows—to protect your assets.

★ ★ ★   STRATEGY 42   ★ ★ ★

WIN THE BATTLE FOR BUREAUCRATIC HILL. Bureaucracy is a significant part of the great game of life. Your effectiveness as a human being will be tested by how well you play this game. Bureaucrats thrive on wearing out opponents, so you'll have to be relentless. Take notes. Create the occasional crisis; bureaucrats hate to admit it, but crisis is what gets them going. Strike while the iron is hot, and don't be shy about going to the top when it's warranted—or suggesting that you might.

The Philosophy of Winning

Your tactics reflect your strategy, values, and desired endstate. It all comes back to this: What is winning for you?

It's a philosophic question—and an important one.

We sometimes chafe at the idea of winning in career, relationships, or life. That's understandable.

But there are situations where we're going for the win, times when we know we're right, when the goal is clear, and when we feel we're in competition. That's when strategy and tactics come into play. Often, if we play fair, these situations still turn out win-win for all parties involved.

Anytime career tactics come into play there's always the issue of form versus substance. Is it better to look good or be good? Should an apple polisher polish a rotten apple?

There is something admirable about people who look a mess, act a mess, and are otherwise dedicated and competent in their careers. And there's something revolting about those who look and act professional but are uninvolved with anything other than their own advancement. We see both types in the military, but rarely does either type advance to "be-all-you-can-be" level.

The successful individual has both pieces—form and substance.

The ethical considerations of the equation are always present. It's something we all have to work through, each in our own way. We'll demonstrate the answers in our values, strategy, and tactics.

Train Tough Challenge

List the life skill tactics that have occurred to you while reading this chapter.

_____

_____

_____

What are some of the moral and ethical considerations involved in employing these tactics?

_____

_____

_____

14

★

HEALTH

Choose or Lose

Fit soldiers can call on their minds and bodies to perform strenuous activity for extended periods and return to normal effectiveness after a relatively short period of rest.
—Army Field Manual 22-100

OK, choose or lose is simplistic. I admit it. Many people struggle with disease or the effects of accidents through no fault of their own. They're genuine victims. Life is random like that. It's unfair. But it doesn't give the rest of us an excuse to ignore the reality that the majority of health problems are self-inflicted.

Sure, it's easier to do nothing and hope for the best. If you're looking for exceptions and excuses they're easy to find.

It's easy to eat doughnuts. There's a drive-through doughnut shop a half mile from my neighborhood. It's cheap and convenient; the staff is friendly and accommodating. The doughnuts are great, and sometimes they slip an extra into the box—a baker's dozen.

It's easy.

Across the state line liquor stores were recently opened on Sunday for the first time. Naturally, the television crews were on hand to interview the first customers. Do I need to describe these happy campers? Or can you already picture them in your mind? Hallelujah. Buying liquor was just made easier.

Hey, that's great. I'm all for personal choice. The nice thing about a liquor store is that you can pick up a carton of cigarettes and buy a lotto ticket in the same stop. Maybe pick up a racy mag and some high-calorie snacks. Very convenient.

Health, on the other hand, is a choice. You have to choose to stand up to what's considered normal.

It's a war—75 percent of the diseases of the western hemisphere are lifestyle related. So there are a lot of casualties. Diddly-bopping down life's highway can get you killed.

We're fighting twenty-first-century temptations with Stone Age bodies. The bodies we live in today were built for physical activity and unprocessed food. We're genetically programmed to like the taste of fat and to binge-eat. It's true. Early humans never knew where their next meal was coming from, so they pigged out whenever they could and stored the excess. We're up against our own biology here.

If you grew up in a home where Mama stuffed you full of pudding and soda and sat you down in front of the TV, you have a special challenge. Unhealthy behaviors are learned. And if you never learned healthy behaviors, like exercise, they're going to be that much tougher to install now.

For most of us, health is the mother of all battles.

It's simple, but it's not easy.

The health challenge is different for each of us. Our genetic programming is unique, our upbringing is unique, and our personalities and willpower vary. That's why there are thousands of books and programs on the subject, and different strokes for different folks.

Maintaining a healthy body weight is going to be easier for some folks than for others. We each have hundreds of genetic elements associated with body weight alone.

Exercise is going to come more easily to those who grew up in an active family than to those who grew up in a sedentary environment.

I can't help that.

We can't go back and unscrew your gene pool either—at least not yet.

The day is coming when the biotechnocrats will be able to help us with a lot of this.

In the meantime we've got to play the hand dealt to us as best we can.

We've got to choose.

That's why I say it's simple, but it's not easy.

It's a simple choice, but a hard road to follow. And the road is different for every human being.

Fortunately, you've got a major ally in the fight: a twenty-first-century brain.

That's right. You may have a Stone Age body and a so-so gene pool, but your mind is in the twenty-first century and has access to twenty-first-century knowledge and techniques. Your mind is the one thing you've got with which to outthink the challenge.

Motivation. Discipline. Sacrifice. Confidence. You're going to need the full arsenal of victory to get to the next level of a healthy life. Organization. Problem solving. Teamwork. Execution. The combat business model is perfectly tailored to assist in the fight.

But nothing we do here can possibly relieve you of the responsibility to think.

Health is a mind-set. It's a choice—the choice to break down bad habits and replace them with good.

There is no miracle pill. You'll to have to commit resources, including time and energy, in order to change habits. You'll need a plan. Your plan.

The Right Use of Shock

The key to a healthy life is motivation. We used to view motivation as coming from the heart, but, of course, it actually comes from the human brain—it's part of the thinking process. Motivation is mental.

One of the challenges in building health is that we take it for granted. It's pretty hard to tell an eighteen-year-old, "If you keep that up, you're going to kill yourself." An eighteen-year-old has no concept of mortality. Even if others are dying around him, his psyche is telling him, "It won't happen to me." It's how we're programmed. Nature spurs young people to live with reckless abandon.

Similarly, the concept of health is vague for a lot of people. We take it for granted, or health is seen as random, something that falls apart out in the future. A jelly doughnut is tangible; it's now. It's immediate. It's gratifying. And it has a fancy name—*immediate gratification.*

Let's face it, success in any endeavor means overcoming the immediately gratifying. An athlete doesn't party the night before a game. A savings account is made up of dollars that could have been spent on other things. Marriages are based on commitment.

An athlete knows the penalty for the ill-timed party. She won't be at her best for the game. Sure, some people are so far above their competition that they can get away with it. But the vast majority of successful athletes have disciplined themselves for peak performance. Defeat is a very real possibility for an athlete, enough to help her forgo the party.

Wealth is disciplined money. And there's no amount of money that can't be blown. We could all quadruple our lifestyles, live high for a couple years, and crash. The thought of crashing keeps us disciplined.

Like any call to action, health decisions respond to the right use of shock.

The key is to experience shock in its nonlethal mode, blow it up large, and harness it.

Don't wait until the doctor tells you that you have three months to live.

Spur yourself now, while there's still time. Make it sting. Then look for little spurs to keep you moving in the right direction.

My spur to action came in June 1981, as a student officer at Fort Benjamin Harrison, Indiana.

As an athlete I always maintained myself in good physical condition, but an ankle injury sidelined me for several months. For the first time in my life, I fell seriously out of shape.

The school commandant was a fitness bug who took the whole school on a long formation run every week. I couldn't hack it. It was hot, my ankle hurt, my resolve weakened, and I fell out.

The commandant had a special program for fallouts: the straggler platoon.

All the stragglers were gathered up and assembled outside a small stadium, where our grand entrance was awaited with much pomp and circumstance. We took one lap around the track as our cohorts, having finished their run, applauded our efforts. Guidons circled us in mock celebration. We passed in review, right under the nose of the commandant himself.

I have to give him credit—he fired me up. From that day forward I was on a mission.

Physical fitness became a way of life. By the end of my course I was maxing the Army Physical Training Test, something I would continue to do the rest of my career.

Humiliation was the spur. It stuck in my craw and motivated me to take action. Fortunately, the Army provided a structure and facilities to maximize my efforts.

And that's important.

Your spur has to be harnessed. Spurring a horse in the wild just leads to a wilder horse. The horse's energy has to be harnessed for maximum effect. You have to have a plan.

And it has to be *your* plan.

The remainder of this chapter will get you thinking. It's not a plan. For it to be effective, you have to devise your own plan. The individual thinking process makes all the difference. Others can help, but no one can do it for you.

Check out the end of this chapter. It's there to facilitate your list—all the little things you can think of to move you in a healthy direction. As you generate ideas, write them down. Take ownership.

Most of the things you write down you already know to do. Now you must commit to doing them.

A healthy lifestyle is rarely about knowledge. Most of what we need to know we learned in eighth-grade health class. The challenge is acting on the knowledge.

For instance, it makes eminent good sense to take a daily multivitamin. It ensures you're getting the vitamins you need that you might otherwise miss in your diet.

Do I have to run down all the vitamins and what they do in order to make the case?

Do we really have to go into the liquid vitamin debate?

Is it necessary to make it a chemistry class and break down the process to it's molecular structure?

Just take the damn vitamin.

Every day. It's a no-brainer.

Do the basics. Start with the fundamentals.

If you want to become a vitamin expert there are hundreds of books on the subject.

The point is, most of what you need to know on the subject of health you already know.

The problem is not knowledge. The problem is motivation.

You have to shock yourself. And you need a plan to harness your new-found motivation.

Let's get you thinking. Jot down your bright ideas at the back of the chapter as we move along. Then invent your own plan.

And commit to making it work.

Develop an Active Lifestyle

Drive onto any military base and you'll see we're into an active lifestyle. Get there early in the morning, and the troops will be running. Go to the gym at noon and they'll be shooting hoops or lifting weights. Stop by in the evening and we'll be playing softball under the lights. And that's when we're not humping rucksacks on a road march. The system is designed to foster an active lifestyle, because regardless of how sophisticated war becomes, we want to have the physical edge on our opponents.

The first rule of an active lifestyle is contained in the three words Sergeant Carter shouted at Gomer Pyle: "MOVE! MOVE! MOVE!"

The how and where was never as important as the fact that Pyle was moving. That's the way it is with an active lifestyle—there are a million ways to get moving. Try them out. Experiment. Look for variety. But keep moving.

Living an active life will make you an elite American. Over 60 percent of Americans don't get enough exercise, and a quarter don't do any at all. Sporting goods sales are down, as is participation in team and recreational sports. And we wonder why dissatisfaction with our bodies is up.

If it were easy, everybody would do it. But it's not. Not nearly as easy as watching TV and playing video games.

You've got to get jacked up.

It takes motivation. It takes energy. It takes discipline—even doing things when you don't want to. For most of us, that's a truly novel concept.

But if you wait till you're in the mood, it will never happen. You've got to change your mood.

Put on some music and get juiced.

Plan for variety. You can't keep doing the same exercises over and over again ad infinitum. It's too boring and can actually lead to stress injuries. Your body needs different kinds of challenges to reach full potential. Everything points to the importance of variety.

Still, some things are fundamental.

Warm up and stretch. The older we get, the more warm-up and stretch time is required. Flexibility is important, but it takes work.

Get that heart rate up. I'm talking aerobic exercise: running, swimming, cycling—choose your torture. If you can make it fun, so much the better, but aerobic exercise usually feels a lot like hard work. And you need to be getting some most every day. Yes, some days can be light days when you do some kick-ass housework or brisk walking, but with the exception of an occasional rest day, keep moving. It will pay off in a stronger and more efficient body, decreased weight, and lowered exposure to diabetes and cardiovascular disease.

Do you know anybody with diabetes? It's a royal pain. With cardiovascular disease we're talking heart attack. These aren't just words, we're talking about the opportunity to avoid some really bad things.

But you're not done yet. You need to do strength training. You're going to replace fat with muscle; strengthen joints, ligaments, and tendons; and prevent degenerative diseases like osteoporosis. You want to get buff.

But don't try to do it all at once. Build, my friend, build. Establish a base. Let us have no heart attacks or strokes here. Go slow when starting something new; excessive soreness will only set you back. Work push-ups and sit-ups into your repertoire. We teach them in the military because they save money on equipment, and we find we can pack them up and take them wherever we go.

Strength training should be an every-other-day activity. Your muscles need about forty-eight hours to recover.

Work the large muscles first. Lift and return weights slowly, to put stress on muscle, not on joints. The more momentum you generate, the less muscle is used. So go slow. Inhale when bringing weight toward your body; exhale when moving the weight away.

Build up to peak performance, the point in your workout at which you're working to muscle failure. This is where you're getting the most benefit. Then reduce the weight, and work back down.

Time your workouts and keep to a schedule. Set goals. Once in a while have a breakthrough session where you push yourself and reach a new level of intensity. Then take a day or two off.

Keep trying new things; don't get bored.

Like a good military unit, you want to keep yourself in the band of excellence—that range where you're always in shape. You lose 80 percent of conditioning after four weeks of inactivity, a place you don't want to go. It would take a month of hard work to get back where you were.

Consistency is key. Constancy of purpose is another.

Keep track. Chart progress. Identify specific goals.

But get started. Working out makes you better. It builds confidence. It's a triumph over laziness and procrastination.

Don't worry about perfection. Fat and fit is still better than fat with no exercise.

Thinking about losing weight? There are a lot of ways to go about that process—but maintaining weight loss always includes an active lifestyle.

★ ★ ★ **STRATEGY 43** ★ ★ ★

"MOVE! MOVE! MOVE!" Develop an active lifestyle. If it were easy, everybody would be doing it. But it's not. It takes aerobic exercise— like running, swimming, or cycling—to get that heart rate up. Keep trying new things; don't get bored. Keep track. Chart progress. Identify specific goals. Activity makes you better, and it builds confidence. It's a triumph over laziness and procrastination.

The Battle of Diet and Weight Control

Rushing into battle will get you killed.

We tried that in Korea in 1950 when the North Koreans stormed across the thirty-eighth parallel. We threw together a task force of occupation troops from Japan and hoped for the best. There were those who thought the sight of Americans would sober up the North Koreans. It didn't happen.

"Task Force Smith" was a group of fine young Americans who were thrown into the breach, but who never had a chance.

During the downsizing of the 1990s, the Army had a motto: "No More Task Force Smiths!" We decided that no matter how lean our force became, we were never going to allow ourselves to have to fight like that again. Winging it is very costly on the battlefield.

A plan is much better. Something like what MacArthur did later in the war—swing around behind the enemy with an amphibious assault and attack from the rear. Cut off his supply lines. Put him on the defensive. Get him out in the open where you can destroy him in detail.

That's the kind of plan you need. A plan that has a basic understanding of your enemy. A plan that wrests the initiative, that you can execute violently.

You're going into battle. No doubt about it. The system is out to get you. The culture is designed to make you fat. Our culture takes physical activity out of life—from the way suburbs are designed, to elevators and escalators, to TV and video games. Fast food is high-calorie and addictive, as is a lot of the packaged, processed foods we buy in supermarkets. Restaurants keep going to larger and larger portions and buffets. Let's put it this way: If you're just rolling along with the culture, you don't have a chance.

Your plan must recognize *your* enemy. Your enemy is different from my enemy. My enemy is fast food and large portions. Your enemy may be sweets and inactivity. Know your enemy, so you can focus your fire. You don't want to be firing indiscriminately all over the battlefield. Eventually you just run out of ammo. It's much more effective to find a good target and blow the heck out of it.

Your plan must wrest the initiative. That means attacking. You can't just hunker down. You've got to get out in front of the problem and kill bad guys before they get in the foxhole with you. You can only kill so many bad guys in hand-to-hand combat. It's much easier to kill them with long-range artillery before they even get close.

Are you with me? Am I making any sense?

I hope so, because you're going to have to execute *violently*.

What would it take for you to get up out of your chair, go to the pantry or refrigerator, and throw out something that's a negative in your battle with weight control?

What would it take?

Maybe it's a bag of potato chips. Strew those chips on the back lawn. If anybody asks, you're just feeding the birds.

Maybe it's a doughnut. "Oh, I was just checking to see if this toilet is functioning properly."

You don't have to cause a scene. But you do need to get in the mind-set of violent execution. You're in a battle here, and you're going to have to fight.

By now you should have some notes at the back of this chapter. You're formulating a plan. A plan of action, not just reaction.

Look, effective diet and weight control is not rocket science. You can make it complicated if you want to, but at its core it's very simple: Burn more calories than you take in.

I mean, a space shuttle launch is really, really complicated. You don't just launch a rocket on a whim. By it's very nature it's complicated.

But people have been building and maintaining strong, nice-looking physiques for centuries.

The knowledge base for diet and weight control is not that great. Virtually anybody can grasp the essentials. It's one of those things in life that's 10 percent knowledge and 90 percent motivation. Sure, the nuances can make a difference at the competitive level, but getting to the competitive level also requires a lot of motivation—and organization.

Almost like a military operation, diet and weight control efforts consist of three phases: planning, execution, and assessment.

Planning. Building and maintaining a healthy body requires a strategy, fitted to your unique circumstances and challenges. Even if you can afford professional help in designing this strategy, you're still going to have to buy in. This is one of those things you have to do for yourself.

Planning is critical, and your plan must be aggressive. You have to see into the future, anticipate challenges, and begin acting on them before they're in the foxhole with you.

Since the major dietary challenge facing Americans is losing weight, we'll focus on the weight loss challenge. But you can easily adjust fire for your particular situation.

Let's start with clothing. If you're serious about losing weight, consider the impact that weight loss will have on your wardrobe. Identify clothes you will soon be able to fit into again, and those that you will no longer need. Get rid of the big sizes and expandable waistbands. Buy some new stuff that will fit where you want to be.

Shopping is critical. Plan your trips to the grocery store, and don't shop when you're hungry. Keep your list—just put different items on it. What you buy at the grocery store is what you're going to eat. So it starts there.

Build a supportive environment. Clear the refrigerator and pantry of temptation. I hate the idea of throwing away food, but this is one of those times when radical action is required. Give the nonperishables to a food bank.

Think through all your eating habits, to include dining out. Avoid fast food by packing healthy food instead. Steer clear of buffets—the other steers will thank you for it. Plan ahead for celebrations, all 365 of them. Learn to celebrate with friends and family, not with massive amounts of food.

The key to disciplined eating is deciding what you're going to eat, and how much, before you start eating.

Execution. You've established a high level of commitment, and you have a plan. Now it's time to execute, to live out the minute-by-minute journey of discipline. It won't be easy—or perfect—but your plan reduces temptation to a manageable level. It gives you a chance to succeed.

You're going to have some cravings. We're hardwired for food, and a lifetime of habit exerts a strong pull.

Soldier through the first three days. Tough through all those first impulses.

After three days, the cravings will subside. I find that if I can restrain myself from fast food for three days, I'm past the physical need. The challenge with things like fat and sugar is that the more we eat, the more we want.

You don't have to starve yourself. Just cut portion size and second helpings. The beauty of cutting second helpings is that thirds and fourths disappear as well.

Eat breakfast, even if you're not especially hungry in the morning.

Acquire new tastes—such as skim milk. After a week you won't know the difference.

Think low fat, high fiber. Avoid processed foods.

Increase fruits and vegetables, whole grains, beans, and nonfat dairy. Get out of cookies, cakes, chips, fries, pizza, and candy. Avoid dense foods. Eat stuff that has water and takes up space but doesn't add a lot of calories—like soup.

Go to smaller bites of food. Eat slowly—chew. Focus. Turn off the TV while eating. Distraction detracts from the fulfillment of eating, causing you to eat more.

Alcohol at mealtime is your worst enemy. It will break down your resistance every time.

Drink lots of water instead. It will fill you up and it offers a whole range of health benefits.

We could go into a number of nutrition issues, but we've actually solved most of them already. We haven't messed with any of the basic food groups we learned about in junior high, other than to downsize portions and redistribute.

Take that multivitamin at breakfast, and add other vitamin supplements as you see fit.

Keep adding to your list of techniques as you move forward. You're in charge.

Assessment. Do a lot of assessment, especially at the beginning. What worked? Where did you slip up?

Failure is not a dirty word. *Quitting* is a dirty word.

Hey, it's war. And there are going to be casualties and difficulties. A set-back isn't cause to lose control.

Adjust fire. Keep score. Chart progress.

Add to your list of techniques. Little things mean a lot in the battle of the bulge.

For most of us, diet and exercise boil down to burning more calories than we take in.

Be realistic. You're building a system here. It's going to take time. Persist.

★ ★ ★   **STRATEGY 44**   ★ ★ ★

WIN THE BATTLE OF DIET AND WEIGHT CONTROL. Recognize your enemies, and build a plan to defeat them. Beer, doughnuts, and pizza come to mind. Build a supportive environment. Clear the refrigerator and cupboards of temptation. Shop carefully. Acquire new tastes. Cut portion sizes and second helpings. Eliminate alcohol at mealtime; it will break down your resistance every time. Drink plenty of water instead. Soldier through the first three days of your plan. Remember, *failure* is not a dirty word, *quitting* is a dirty word.

Take the Night Off

Good news. It's not all diet discipline and workouts; good health thrives on rest and relaxation. We just have to remember how to rest and relax, to harken back to a carefree period in our lives when it all seemed to operate on cruise control.

Americans work harder and longer than anyone in the industrialized world. It's easy to lose perspective—and sleep. We're sweating the small stuff.

For most of us, rest and relaxation take planning; otherwise, they get crowded out by the ever escalating tempo of operations. "Optempo" we call it in the military.

When a unit is driving hard and optempo is high, we know to identify periods when we can slow it down, and make time for rest. High-speed units schedule numerous "training holidays," or days when the entire unit can stand down for some rest and relaxation.

Every soldier, sailor, airman, and marine—from buck private to four-star general—gets thirty paid vacation days a year. We want our people to be there when we need them, and to be somewhere having fun when we don't. We've learned the value of keeping people fresh.

We've also learned that people need sleep. That may seem intuitively obvious, but when you're training people to think they're ten feet tall, it's easy to forget about sleep.

That's why we have sleep plans. Yes, we actually plan sleep.

What we found was that units were doing seventy-two-hour continuous training exercises without sleep. By the end of the exercise, the leaders were walking into trees and generally making poor decisions. We discovered that when soldiers are physically tired, their creative and logical functions were dead long before. What a great time for the enemy to attack.

So we changed all that.

Now we design sleep plans to make sure everyone gets the rest they need to remain functional. Training is still tiring and stressful, but it's also realistic. War doesn't stop every seventy-two hours, and neither can our soldiers. We found that with planning, we can go longer, more effectively.

If we can do it, you can do it.

Determine how many hours of sleep you need each night to be at your best the next day. For the vast majority of people, it's seven or eight hours.

Then cut out the extraneous stuff in your life that's keeping you from your optimal amount of sleep. Sometimes it's nothing more than breaking the late-night TV habit.

Develop a sleep routine. Go to bed at the same time each night. Sleep in a dark, well-ventilated room, on a firm mattress. Eliminate alcohol, caffeine, and a full stomach from the equation.

Good sleep is part art and part science. It's worth the investment, because sleep is like fuel—if you're expending massive amounts of energy during the day, you need an equivalent amount of sleep at night.

If you spend any amount of time around kids, you know I am not making this up. You can gauge the amount of sleep kids are getting by how they act during the day. There was only one thing I asked of parents when I coached youth sports: Get the kid a good night's sleep the night before a game. I could always tell who was doing sleepovers on game night—those kids were worthless the next day.

Sleep is absolutely essential for maintaining a positive attitude and emotional well-being. Small wonder that we're now discovering the long-term health benefits of sleep as well.

Build yourself a good rest and relaxation plan. Make time to renew. You'll feel better for it.

★ ★ ★ STRATEGY 45 ★ ★ ★

GET MORE SLEEP. Most of the fifty strategies emphasize hard work and fighting your way out of a comfort zone. Now I'm telling you, emphatically, to get into your comfort zone and get more sleep. The vast majority of people need seven or eight hours a night—and we're not getting it. The right amount of sleep is essential for maintaining a positive attitude and emotional well-being. Build yourself a rest and relaxation plan. Develop a sleep routine, and make time to renew.

The Lifestyle Makeover

There was a time when a soldier could count on free cigarettes in his pack of C rations. We sold them dirt cheap at the commissary. Cheap cigarettes were a benefit of military service.

As long as a guy could stay out of jail and show up sober for duty, alcoholism was often overlooked.

Physical conditioning was lax in peacetime, and weight control was a matter between a soldier and the discretion of his commanding officer. The standards varied, and we had a lot of seriously overweight soldiers waddling around.

We were tolerating, and in some cases encouraging, a lifestyle that was counterproductive to the well-being of our force. The leading causes of death in America have always been tobacco, poor diet and lack of exercise, and alcohol. We were flirting with all three, and our sick rates, serious incident rates, and absenteeism reflected it.

The cost-benefit analysis cried out for a healthier force. It took time, but we turned things around, gradually turning up the heat on the old habits while offering healthful, fun alternatives. In the end we executed a revolutionary cultural makeover, one step at a time. Today's force is far, far healthier than at any time in our history.

If we can do it, you can too.

Health is the ultimate choice. It's a mind-set, a series of carefully embedded habits.

In the military we decided it was unfair of us to demand individual action when the culture we were providing did not support that action. We wanted a healthy force, but we were providing an unhealthy environment. So we changed the culture.

Health is a choice, but healthful actions are executed within a culture. Your family can either be a support network or a stumbling block. Chances are they'll be much more supportive if they know what's going on. So tell them. Ask for support. It's the rare spouse who'll say, "Actually, I was just thinking we should smoke and drink more, and maybe add a few more pounds of flab."

I'm absolutely convinced that Americans know what's healthy and what's not. The challenge is not education, it's motivation.

We have to recognize the dangers of where our unconscious decisions are taking us. Then we can examine these decisions in the light of day, and choose to change.

Get started.

Destroy a couple unhealthy habits, and replace them with healthy ones. Then look for more worlds to conquer. Build. Good habits build on each other and become mutually reinforcing.

The gratification may not be immediate, but you'll see and feel the results in time. That's where discipline comes in. And sacrifice. And confidence.

It's been done before.

You can do it too.

Train Tough Challenge

Here's space for writing down your ideas for a healthier lifestyle. Jot them down as they come to you. Stay focused!

_____

_____

_____

_____

_____

15

★

WEALTH

Leveraging the Military Mind

There is no security on this earth; there is only opportunity.
—General Douglas MacArthur

J oining the United States Military is a lifestyle choice.

There are limited hair and wardrobe options. You don't get rich, but there are plenty of financial benefits and advantages that come with military service. Medical. Dental. Education. Tax breaks. Inexpensive life insurance. Thirty days' paid vacation. Generous retirement. Burial.

Kids could be born into a military family, sign up on their own after high school or college, serve until retirement, and hence go cradle to grave in the system.

It's a business decision. You look at salary and allowances, the longevity pay raises, and the opportunity for promotion. Joining makes you part of an extended family, and offers you a rung on the hierarchy. The amenities increase as you advance. Everybody knows fairly precisely how everybody else is doing; compared to American society at large, the disparities are minimal.

The system is there to protect you. There are no missed paychecks.

Every two or three years, you're going to pack up and move. You could go from Hawaii to Alaska; from Germany to Korea. California to Kansas to Alabama to New Jersey. Or vice versa.

You adjust your lifestyle to the opportunities at each location.

At the end of a career you've had the benefit of a steadily increasing salary and numerous opportunities to reinvent your life with each change in location.

The question is: What are the lessons learned from this lifestyle?

As Americans we love to study the lives of Rockefeller, Trump, and Gates—entrepreneurs with unique talents, unquenchable drives, and larger-than-life lifestyles. Or we focus on the talented—the Jordans, Streisands, and Snoop Doggy Doggs.

There's a lot to learn from these folks, though it's actually of marginal use. In point of fact, the incremental wealth accumulation of the military system more closely approximates the security to which most Americans aspire.

Let's take a look at the military mind-set on wealth, and see what nuggets remain to be mined from the vast mother lode of financial advice that confronts us at every turn.

Security and Risk

The wild card in every military career is the ever present possibility of being shot at by bad guys. Our situation can change into a very bad thing, very quickly.

That's the big risk we take, and it's about all the risk we really want. We'd like the rest of the stuff of life to be as secure and predictable as possible. That's why our reward and support system is structured the way it is.

We do a risk assessment for every operation. We want to know the dangers and the odds of success or failure. This process naturally extends to how we think about wealth and money management.

Two principles of warfighting are especially germane: security and simplicity.

Security is critical. The first thing we do after achieving an objective is set up security. We know the enemy likes to hit us when we're overconfident, before our guard is up. So we've learned over time to make security a habit. Complacency is a deadly fault in our business. Good leaders never underestimate the deviousness of the enemy.

The battles we face are not unlike the war for your dollar.

Secure what's yours.

The assault on your money is persistent and insidious. The economy is fueled by spending, and the full array of marketing and advertising is designed to separate you from your money. Hey, it's a great system, as long as you're playing it, and it's not playing you.

Defend.

If something sounds too good to be true, it is.

Develop a bullshit detector. Bad things, like rats, smell.

Be leery of professionals. Professional advice is one thing; handing over your money for uses you don't completely understand is another.

Take a look at the odds on lotteries and gambling. Get out of the mindset that relies on luck and getting something for nothing.

Learn the power of *no*.

Protect and defend.

This is not a hunker-down mentality. We're still going to exploit opportunity—after we check it out.

Keep things simple.

Simplicity is another key principle of warfighting that applies to financial management.

All things being equal, the simple plan is best. It eases understanding, communication—and execution. In war we seldom undertake what we haven't mastered. Plans that look great on paper must also stand up to the realities of combat.

A simple lifestyle also has advantages, as many military families have learned. When you have to pack up and move every few years, you have an added incentive to keep material acquisitions within reason—and to periodically clean house. In our world, lean is better.

Develop a Philosophy of Wealth

Examine what you really think and feel about wealth, and see if the general direction of your life supports your reasoned conclusions. Too often we find ourselves obsessing in this area, without thinking about why we feel the way we do.

I work very hard in this area of my life, and it's a constant struggle to stay rational. I've never been poor, but I've seen others in poverty. I've only been broke once, and that was in prep school when somebody pinched the cash I kept in my dresser drawer. Being broke was a temporary situation; being poor is a state of mind.

I've always had a healthy regard for the value of a dollar, but I've spent time with people for whom money was no object. They could instantly solve many of life's nasty little problems simply by throwing excessive amounts of money at them. Money was like toilet paper for these people. It was an impressive display and, I must say, a lot of fun. No table at the club? How much would it take to make one instantly appear, right up front? That kind of thing.

Money isn't everything, but it's clear the problems of poor people are more daunting than the problems of the rich. That may seem intuitively obvious, until you consider the boredom and disappointment that often accompany life for the rich and famous. After all, surveys say that once Americans have their basic necessities provided for, they have as much chance of claiming happiness as the rich. Believe me, rich people are not walking around in a constant state of euphoria.

No matter how far ahead some people seem to be, life on earth has its equalizers. Everybody gets to age, have bowel movements—and die. The random stuff hits rich and poor alike. There are some things you just can't buy your way out of.

Unfortunately, people make comparisons. Wealth becomes relative, a matter of perception. If we're not careful, our well-being has meaning only in comparison to those better, or less well off, than ourselves.

Fight this attitude. Resist it tooth and nail. Shut out the media if necessary. Avoid those for whom one-upmanship is a way of life. Count your blessings. Name them one by one.

What's important to you? What is wealth for you? What do you value?

If you say you value something, ask yourself, "What have I done about it?"

If you're not acting on your values, go back and reevaluate. You may be kidding yourself.

Get to know yourself in this area, and accept that your conclusions will be different from the next person's. We value different things. And we definitely have different risk tolerances.

Entrepreneurs tend to be more at ease with the ups and downs of life, more confident living on the edge. Savers are more risk averse, forgoing some of life's pleasures for a nest egg and the feeling of security.

There is no right and wrong in this arena, only what's right for you.

There's no right amount of debt, right amount of income, or right amount of savings. There's only what's right for you, what you're comfortable with.

But there is stupid.

There is saying one thing and doing another. There is letting life beat you about the head and shoulders, ignoring the basic rules of the game, only to pay the price in penalties.

And there is wisdom. Knowing yourself. Knowing the rules. Playing the game ethically, confidently, and with an attitude of constant learning.

Know what you want. Appreciate and protect what you have. Understand your tolerance for risk. Become a student of the rules of the game, as you choose to play it.

★ ★ ★ **STRATEGY 46** ★ ★ ★

DEVELOP A PHILOSOPHY OF WEALTH. Know where you fit on the security-versus-risk spectrum. Know yourself and what your challenges are in thinking about, defining, and acquiring wealth. Know what you want. Appreciate and protect what you have. If you say you value something, ask yourself, "What am I doing about it?" If you're not acting on your values, go back and reevaluate.

The Rules of the Game

Think of money management as a board game, where you move around the board somewhat randomly, perhaps by a roll of the dice. You can't anticipate everything, or the order in which every event will occur, but by consistently making wise decisions you significantly enhance your chances for success.

In any game, there are primary components. In the military we have the Army, Navy, Air Force, and Marines. For us to be successful we have to get the most out of each component, and synchronize their efforts.

Money management has components as well. A working knowledge of each component will maximize your effectiveness. This gives you balance—just what you need for handling the randomness of life. Balance helps you weather the tough situations and take full advantage of opportunity.

Consider the following components as you think about money management.

Insurance. Insure for the big stuff; don't sweat the small stuff. Your life, health, income, house, and car are the primary concerns.

How important are your life and income to the welfare of your family? How will they fare in the event of your demise? A reasonable amount of life insurance is a smart bet to cover this worst-case contingency. Watch out for bells and whistles when purchasing life insurance. Skip the accidental death and waiver of premium options, and just buy life insurance—keep your financial investments separate.

Health insurance is a must—and watch out for your kids as they age out of eligibility for your family plan. Insist that they take out coverage on themselves. You can bet they'll come running to you in the event they need help with hospital bills.

Keep deductibles high on your house and car. Again, you can self-insure for those amounts and almost certainly save money in the long run.

Drop collision and comprehensive when the value of your car is less than ten times the annual premium. Know the ropes of which driver to assign to which car, and the discounts and credits for which you qualify. Make sure every driver in the family understands the financial ramifications of driving violations and accidents. It's more than they think.

Finally, protect your financial assets with adequate liability insurance, so if you conk some guy with a golf ball, you're covered.

Saving and Spending. These two are intimately related, and you need a plan for both.

Save at least 5 percent of your monthly income, and have the money deducted from your paycheck and invested before it hits your hot little hand. Saving is an acquired taste. Try it, and after a while you'll like it.

Have a spending plan, and spend less than you make. In the military we keep a decrement list, a prioritized list of projects we fund as money becomes available. It works at the personal level too, providing a realistic picture of the expenses ahead, and helping us stay focused when the impulse buy beckons. Instead of thinking in terms of things you can "afford," think about your priorities. Make your spending decisions based on these priorities.

Spending in some areas yields dividends; spending in others is double jeopardy. Buying a house provides you with not only a place to live, but a chance to see some appreciation. Spending on cigarettes costs more than money; there are also the health effects to take into account. Consider the total cost of things, not just the price.

Understand the cost of debt, especially credit card debt. It's generally better to pay off credit card debt, even if you have to dip into savings to do it. Sacrifice if you have to. Then instill the discipline to stay out of high-costing debt.

Investments. We're dumber than we think in this area. The studies all show it: Human beings have a very limited capacity to digest information and make complex decisions. We tend to do false forecasting, projecting what's coming next based on incomplete information. Humility is in order here. Your system for beating the stock market is probably a pipe dream.

Few of us have the time or tools to intelligently pick stocks, much less to time the highs and lows. Market timers tend to panic with the pack, and overreact to the pain of loss.

The key is to build a system that takes advantage of the long-term trend.

Over the long haul, the U.S. stock market has been a very lucrative vehicle in which to invest. Think about it: What better place to invest than in the business of the United States of America? Despite recent scandals, the United States provides a stable system of laws and government in a country that goes to great pains to protect itself. We're a creative, innovative people, who are unusually open to new ideas and opportunities. I don't know about you, but I'm betting on the ol' United States.

The question is: How, and how much?

My answer to the first part of the question is mutual funds.

I'm neither educated nor interested enough to pick stocks, so mutual funds give me an opportunity to participate in the American dream without kidding myself about my level of expertise. I let the pros do the selection for me. I look for no-load funds with low administrative costs. And I diversify. The Securities and Exchange Commission's forays into the after hours trading in mutual funds just makes me more confident that mutual fund governance will be stronger and more transparent.

I use the Rule of 100 to tell me "how much." Each year I take my age and deduct it from 100. The difference is the percentage I maintain in mutual funds. So at age 45, I had 55 percent of my savings in a variety of mutual funds and 45 percent in safe investments like money markets, certificates of deposit (CDs), and savings bonds. Each year I decrease my exposure to risk, because my ability to invest for the long haul decreases with each passing year.

I use the Rule of 72 to tell me when I can expect my savings to double. A given rate divided into 72 yields the number of years until the money doubles. For instance, your principal will double after nine years at 8 percent. Playing around with this formula for a few minutes will illustrate the importance of even the smallest increase in your rate of return.

Make your money work hard for you, but only at a level of risk you understand and are willing to accept. Invest for the long term, and the odds are in your favor.

Taxes. Tax is the ultimate game, with the rules changing every year. I did my own taxes for thirty years, but eventually the game became too quick for me, and now I have help.

I'm not anal about saving taxes; it's a great country and I'm willing to pay my share. At the same time, there's smart and there's stupid. The system gives tax breaks for certain behaviors, and I try to behave that way whenever possible.

There are great advantages for savers. Saving under the sponsored plans can yield you megabucks, especially over time. Make maximum use of these programs.

The system rewards spending for education, so not only do you have the pleasure of learning and the benefit of an expanded resume, you get a tax break as well.

Buying a house with a mortgage has tax advantages; buying a car on time does not. Since a house generally appreciates and a car does just the opposite, it makes more sense to splurge in the direction of your home, and be modest in your choice of vehicle. Just a thought.

Sin is taxed heavily. Alcohol, tobacco, and gambling get hit hard. Donations to charitable enterprises are usually tax deductible.

Which brings me to my next subject.

★ ★ ★ **STRATEGY 47** ★ ★ ★

THINK OF MONEY MANAGEMENT AS A BOARD GAME. As in any board game, some occurrences are random, and you get penalized for not knowing the rules. You're rewarded for playing your hand wisely. It's imperative to understand the nuances of insurance, saving and spending fundamentals, investing, and taxes. What you don't know will cost you. Decide to become a student of the rules of wealth. Play hard.

Give, Give, Give

The longer I hang around planet Earth, the more I appreciate the importance of giving. Our country is built on what people give—in time, talent, and treasure. The physical evidence can be seen in churches, synagogues, and civic arenas. Sometimes harder to trace is the contribution of charitable and religious foundations. And sometimes completely lost in the shuffle is the tremendous outpouring of assistance that Americans respond with in times of crisis and need.

Consider the North Platte Canteen.

During the heyday of passenger trains, North Platte, Nebraska, was a fifteen-minute stop in the middle of nowhere, a place where trains were serviced. Throughout World War II the trains were packed with American servicemen, often at the midway point of a miserable five-day cross-country journey characterized by dry rations, cramped sleeping quarters, and an uncertain future.

Somebody got the idea to give the boys a break at the North Platte stop, and the canteen was born.

From December 1941 until well past the end of the war, local citizens met the traveling servicemen with sandwiches, eggs, coffee, and cake—all free of charge. It was a gargantuan effort, often with twenty or more trains a day. Townspeople from all over the area pitched in.

A piano was donated. Local girls danced the boogie-woogie with the surprised and newly animated young men. North Platte became an oasis of love and kindness in an otherwise forlorn journey to war.

No one who experienced it would ever be the same. The North Platte Canteen became a subject soldiers and sailors talked about in the darkest hours of war. The people who gave there remembered it as the greatest experience of their lives.

Success at anything takes laser focus, grit, and determination. Sometimes we have to claw our way to the top. It can be a cutthroat, white-water world.

Don't miss the joy of giving something back.

Once in a while, make someone's day. Share the love.

★ ★ ★ **STRATEGY 48** ★ ★ ★

GIVE SOMETHING BACK. The evidence of what our forebears bequeathed to us is everywhere. Don't miss the joy of giving something back. Give. Give. Give. It's an attitude.

Which Brings Us Back to Endstate

What is wealth for you? What is your mission?

What does it look like five, ten, or twenty years down the road? How does it feel?

Reverse plan that destination. Lay out the steps, in reverse order, that you see yourself taking to get there.

How bad do you want it?

Bad enough to ferret out the opportunities your current situation is providing?

Bad enough to discipline yourself and develop the habits requisite to achieving your goals?

Decide to become a student of the rules of wealth. Play hard.

And don't forget to give something back.

Train Tough Challenge

List three immediate actions you will take to impact your financial situation:

1. _____

2. _____

3. _____

What will you give back?

_____

_____

_____

16
―――★―――
RELATIONSHIPS

The Toughest Game in Town

There is no simple formula for success in all the situations you may face.
—Army Field Manual 22-100

I saved the toughest chapter for last. Just because you made it this far doesn't mean you can make it all the way to the end. Here's where it gets tough.

It's a shame, but for a lot of people examining relationships is painful. They'll run through tackle after tackle on a football field and meet with and destroy an enemy in hand-to-hand combat—then run for cover when it comes to relationships.

That's why I call it the toughest game in town. The truth is, relationships, whether personal or professional, have to be worked at like any other human endeavor. In fact, we have to work even harder on relationships if we want them to be successful. Too many people bust their chops in one or two areas of life and leave relationships to take care of themselves.

Some people put forth superhuman effort on the job and then collapse at their own front door as though it were made of kryptonite. Wrong answer.

Close relationships have the greatest power to inflict pain; we ignore them at our peril. The consequences of failure to invest in these closest relationships can be catastrophic. But the fact is that many of us confront our most important relationships when we're at our worst, after a hard day of work.

It's a tough game, and family relationships are the toughest of the tough.

I use "family" in the broadest sense, not just Mom, Dad, 2.5 kids, and a minivan.

Everybody has family issues, even if you're single with no kids and don't know who or where your mother and father are. You still have family issues, albeit different ones.

You can opt out of relationships and family. Climb a mountain and live like a hermit.

You know what?

You're still going to spend a lot of time thinking about relationships—and family.

It's inescapable.

The point is, we're either building relationships and making them stronger, or we're just letting nature take its course.

The challenge is whether to engage, and to what degree.

As you can imagine, we're going all the way to Baghdad on this one. We've come too far to cop out now.

But this is going to really, really hurt.

What in the World Can the U.S. Military Possibly Have to Do with Any of This?

Let me tell you something.

The United States Military has a corner on relationships. You need go no further for the ultimate case study.

Let me tell you why.

Our stock-in-trade is young people who choose to leave home. They volunteer.

There are several reasons why they volunteer: pay and benefits, education, a career, the desire to serve their country. But the bottom line is that they are accepting a total change in relationships. Mom and Dad won't be there. Sissy and Bro aren't going to be there either. Neither are any of the other relationships that Peoria had to offer. Those relationships undergo a major alteration and, in the vast majority of cases, will never be the same.

We're taking on a stressed individual, almost by definition. It's a big responsibility, because we have to provide a support system to assist in this relationship transition. It's also one of the reasons we have relative success in areas like race relations. We take young people out of their previous environment, which sometimes includes prejudice, and place them in an environment where they have to work with and depend on new people. These new people are every color and creed. We work very hard to ensure this new environment is fair and accepting.

It's a tough job, because everything and everyone in the military is transitory. People come and go. Enter stage right, exit stage left. We're going to move these enlistees around the world. They're going to experience a vast array of different people and places.

If they get married, the spouse will join the cruise.

Maybe they'll have kids.

Maybe Dad will leave on deployment or be out at sea for extended periods of time.

Maybe Mom's in the military too.

Maybe one or both will go off to war. It doesn't get much more stressful than that.

A tremendous amount of effort goes into preparing military families to withstand stress. The military community is a uniquely engineered support system. We know that the greater the stress, the better this system has to function.

Venture onto a military base and you'll see numerous buildings and activities prefaced by the word *community*. We foster a sense of community for soldiers and their families—even if it's a temporary stay. Part of the beauty of our support system is that you'll find similar programs at every base in the inventory, worldwide. We're the ultimate extended family.

★ ★ ★ **STRATEGY 49** ★ ★ ★

GIVE YOUR FAMILY SPECIAL ATTENTION. Regardless of how you define family, your family deserves special attention. Amazingly, many of the same techniques that work in the military also work in relationships—and life. Two of these are *organization* and *communication*. Half of the organizational challenge in the American family is simplification. Simplify, simplify, simplify. The challenge in communication is developing the ability to listen. Actions speak louder than words, except for words of praise.

We don't just prepare soldiers for war, we prepare families. We know that a big part of who soldiers are and how they perform is tied up in their relationships. They'll perform better if they know their families are secure and provided for.

We also want soldiers to be able to translate parts of their military training into their relationships—the toughest game in town.

What's So Great About the Great Santini?

Bull Meechum is a Marine fighter pilot. He exhibits many of the qualities we admire in a military man—confidence, energy, organization, personal magnetism. But Bull is a sick puppy—an alcoholic, a braggart, and a bully. He calls himself *The Great Santini*, also the name of the 1979 movie, starring Robert Duval as Bull.

The movie was based on Pat Conroy's book of the same title. Conroy's father was a Marine colonel and Pat is a graduate of The Citadel. Both book and movie are accurate representations of military life.

Bull Meechum runs his family like he runs his squadron, and neither area of his life is going well. His career is capsizing, the result of his eccentric behaviors, and we sense that his military subordinates aren't buying his "hack it or pack it" brand of leadership. Unfortunately, he brings his failed methodologies home.

Lillian, his wife, does an admirable job interpreting Bull's character for their four children, who otherwise find him coldhearted and stifling. She is the perfect complement to his strange brand of leadership, finding love in his various behaviors, and soothing the battered egos he creates at every turn. She ably functions as his sergeant major, checking the children's hair and posture and advising on proper deportment—and handshake procedures.

The teenage children, Ben and Mary Anne, bear the brunt of the gale. Ben is expected to join the Marine Corps, regardless of his personal reservations. On his eighteenth birthday Bull wakes him up at 4:00 A.M. to give him a birthday present—his old leather flight jacket. Their relationship is a series of one-way conversations, with Bull doing the talking. But Ben is finding his place in the world, and gaining ground on his aging father. Bull does not take defeat well; in one heartbreaking scene he repeatedly bounces a basketball off Ben's head.

Mary Anne has a different problem. As a young woman she has no standing in Bull Meechum's world, despite her many efforts to attract his attention. "Can girls be real Meechums?" she asks in frustration.

The Great Santini is an uncomfortable experience. We want to reach out and tweak Bull Meechum, allowing him his military personality and techniques, but opening his mind and the lines of communication to his family. He has his redeeming characteristics—he's a good provider and an entertaining spark plug—but these positives are subsumed by drink and his dog-eat-dog view of the world. Even Lillian can't keep up. She praises where Bull withholds, and she finds love and sensitivity in even his most extreme actions. But it isn't enough.

Only in Bull Meechum's death—he loses his life when he takes his plane out to sea rather than risk crashing it over a town—is the family released from the scourge of his overbearing presence. As they struggle through his funeral and their relocation, we see they have internalized many of Bull's positive attributes. While *The Great Santini* is pure tragedy, it provides great commentary on the pluses and minuses of a military approach to family.

A danger in assessing *The Great Santini* would be to conclude that a dynamic, disciplined, and somewhat driven family must also be drunk and dysfunctional. The negatives don't necessarily follow from the military model. They may be found in all walks of nonmilitary life as well. In fact, traits that succeed or fail in a squadron will have approximately the same effect on a family. Drunkenness fails in both environments. Structure and discipline are pluses in both a squadron and a family. Miscommunication fails in a family, just as it fails in a squadron. The challenge to excel can be positive in a family, just as it is in an elite military unit.

The Great Santini offers an interesting mix of personalities. The Meechums frequently relocate, undergoing the concomitant pressures of adjusting to new surroundings and school environments. It's natural that they adopt some of the features of a Marine squadron, with its inherent toughness, hierarchy, and gung ho attitude.

But Bull Meechum's type A personality takes it over the top. He goes too far. He fails to differentiate between those who have joined the Marines by choice, and those who are merely influenced by the Corps circumstantially. Moreover, Bull's antics fail in the unit just as they fail at home. His alcoholism pushes the envelope, and his escapades degenerate into a nightmare for all concerned.

Great Santini Moments

I admit it. I've had my share of Santini moments. I was probably fortunate to have seen the movie in 1979, the same year my first son was born. It certainly mellowed me out a bit.

When my wife Heidi started bugging me for children I was a second lieutenant. I asked for a staff study. I was doing the math. With every new mouth to feed, there was going to be less for me. Having children was not an entirely rational decision, but I thought it best to approach the issue rationally. So I gave her the format for a military staff study and said, "If having children means so much to you, and you think you can make a case, write it up and we can discuss it." She did, and the case was made.

It was extreme, but the decision to have children is an important one, and the military gave us a logical format in which to consider the option on its merits. Of course, once we got into the execution phase the math went out the window. We have four kids now, and I wouldn't trade the experience for anything.

You can't put a value on watching your boys wrestle at state level or hearing your daughter sing a recital in Italian.

We knew we would sacrifice for our kids, and we have. We counted the cost, which is staggering, and proceeded by faith. We've learned that sacrifice is what makes families possible. We give up some things to share with our kids. I can't drive by a soccer field without thinking how many hours I spent watching or coaching that game. But it came with the territory. Raising a family involves some sacrifice.

Was I a pushy dad?

In some ways, yes.

Heidi and I established standards, and they were enforced.

My type A personality came out in the kids' sports endeavors, where they all endured a few Santini-like lectures along the way. We put systems in place to make sure the kids were better conditioned and better rested than their competition. They were disciplined.

I also don't like to see bored, listless kids. Kids need to be doing something. Sure, they need time to explore, to be with other kids, and to chill out. But after a point they need to be challenged and involved.

Hence, the M. C. Bender Leadership Academy.

The academy was primarily a summer activity, instituted whenever the Bender children appeared to have lost their way. It was a way of providing structure and motivation. Once inside the structure, a kid had tremendous motivation to graduate. And there was no way out but to cooperate and graduate.

The academy featured study and exercise programs, as well as job-skill training. The classics were read. Push-ups were performed to military standards. And whatever needed to be done around the house qualified as job-skill training. It's called *work*.

It wasn't always fun, but there was always something to do.

The Great Santini would have approved.

★ ★ ★   **STRATEGY 50**   ★ ★ ★

WORK FOR BALANCE IN YOUR RELATIONSHIPS. Relationships require constant grooming to survive the pressures of the present culture. Work for balance. There may be times when career demands are going to take precedence over your relationships. Prepare for those times. Organization, teamwork, problem solving, discipline—all the things we've emphasized—will help you through. But, as in everything else, nothing relieves you of the responsibility to think.

Back to Reality

A family is like a military unit, only tighter. Family bonds are unique. There's the genetic piece, and there's also something about functioning in close proximity to people—year after year after year. Family members know the truth about each other, and no matter how dysfunctional they may be, there's always a special bond.

Because of the closeness, it's hard to step back from our family life and ask the basic questions. What's working? What habits do we have? Where are we going? Who's in charge here?

That's why the military model is useful. Military units aren't family, but we do seek to create a family atmosphere. We want our troops to bond and function effectively as a team. Discipline, ethics, problem solving, and teamwork can all be applied to family life. Just add love.

Two areas deserve special attention. They're basic in military units and, if applied correctly, can have a tremendous impact on families.

Organization. A military unit is very focused on organization. Effective organization reduces friction. Things just run more smoothly when we're organized. We maintain duty rosters, calendars, supply and equipment records, and a budget. Everything has its place and everything is checked periodically. It's down to a system. We don't want to be reinventing basic functions, because reinvention is costly, in both time and energy. We sometimes refer to these functions as "housekeeping."

American families have largely lost the systems of organization that came with the family farm. Farm families tended to be large, and organization was a must. There was a structured division of labor, with the big kids helping the little kids and so forth. The routines were established. Projects were broken down into smaller tasks appropriate for the level of the kid performing the task. Farm life was often described as "simple," but it was actually quite complex. It's just that organization made it seem simple.

Today we've replaced function with distraction—in the form of DVD players, video games, and the assorted gadgetry. Instead of *do* more, it's *get* more.

Probably half the required organization in today's family is simplification. Simplify, simplify, simplify.

Getting organized is a dog. It's cultural revolution at its most challenging. Organization requires planning and the persistence to overcome resistance. Ultimately, it becomes a continuous process. Then we call it *maintenance*. The results are reduced friction and the benefits are long term.

It's a great investment.

Communication. Good news here. The most important part of communication is still listening. Not the behind-the-newspaper variety, but active, engaged listening.

Listen to your spouse's predicament, and your kid's exploits. Everybody needs a sounding board, and we ought to be able to find this stress reliever at home.

Remember, criticism is easy. Too often we mistake it for a high-level skill when in actuality any idiot can do it, and idiots often do.

Kids need feedback, but most of it needs to be of the positive variety. Suggest with care.

Kids' sports taught me that the best suggestion is a delayed suggestion. A kid isn't ready for criticism after a less-than-perfect performance. He already has a pretty good idea what his shortcomings were. He's not ready for more input. By delaying your suggestions you're giving him time to air out and allowing your bright ideas to mellow with the test of time. You'll forget the irrelevant criticisms. The good ideas will still be there before his next practice—when he'll be more receptive.

We're building confidence here, so kids need to understand that life includes a lot of do-overs. Excellence is the goal; perfection is only an ideal. Self-esteem is built on struggle, with all its successes and failures. Don't do it all for them. Let them give it a try.

As you can imagine, I'm a great lecturer. Occasionally I can't help myself and the kids get a sermon. It's cathartic, at least for me, but I'm realistic about how much it does for them. Setting an example is probably three-to-one "show" over "tell." I can lecture all day, but my actions carry a lot more weight.

Praise is the one big exception and should rarely be withheld. Too often we hold it in when we should be letting it out. Praise is free, and it's therapeutic for all concerned.

Family members also need to negotiate with each other, and avoid pressing each others' hot buttons during the process.

My daughter Lisa is the master. She knows I'll avoid confrontation if possible, and that anything that sounds like nagging will be counterproductive.

My theory is that the level of desire is directly proportional to the degree of planning that has gone into the request. If you're just whining about something, you really don't want it that badly.

Lisa's adapted to my style. She comes off as direct, rational, and polite. She has decent timing. She makes a good case and accepts compromise. Who could ask for more?

It's not only what we communicate, but how.

Mrs. Great Santini

Almost lost in Robert Duvall's portrayl of Bull Meechum is Blythe Danner playing his wife, Lillian. She does a great job.

Life in the Marine Corps means frequent family moves for Lillian and the four kids. Bull has his redeeming characteristics, but between his drinking and braggadocio he's a roving disaster. Without Lillian, Bull

Meechum has no chance. She's the only person in the movie who understands him and can interpret his behaviors for others. She sees the positive in him, praises him, and is his only fan. In the end, she stands up to him and fights him—that's when we know Bull Meechum has finally gone too far. For a moment even he sees it.

Bull and Lillian have plenty of stress in their traditional relationship. The current reality for many families is even more stressful: Mrs. Santini could be the fighter pilot, or be a single mom. Bull Meechum might be deployed in a combat zone, not just training for it. Instead of the problems of excellence, any of the Meechum kids could be diabetic, bipolar, hyperactive, or have other unique challenges that would impact the family dynamic. Real life is stranger than fiction.

Relationships require constant grooming to survive the pressures of the present culture. The closer and more central the relationship is in your life, the more care is required to nurture it.

Look for balance. There may be times when career demands are going to take precedence over your relationships. Prepare for those times. Organization, teamwork, problem-solving skills, discipline—all the things we've emphasized will help you through.

My drill sergeant had it right when he told me—"It's tough out here, Bender. You won't find the answer on a silver platter. You're going to have to think!"

Train Tough Challenge

List three close relationships.

1. _____

2. _____

3. _____

What single action can you take in each relationship to nudge it in the right direction?

1. _____

2. _____

3. _____

AFTERWORD

Motivating for the Road Ahead

The most terrible job in warfare is to be a second lieutenant leading a platoon when you are on the battlefield.
— General Dwight Eisenhower

I'm writing this from the Eisenhower Suite at Fort Leavenworth, Kansas, a restoration of the apartment in which Ike, wife Mamie, and son John lived during his momentous year attending the Command and General Staff School in 1925–1926.

From this apartment the world changed.

Ike finessed his way into the school and was told by his career advisers in the War Department he "would probably fail."

Prior to arriving he was a little-known officer, viewed as someone who had missed his chance in the Great War, a guy frittering away precious career time coaching football teams.

All that turned around when Ike graduated number one in his class of 245 officers, an event he would later call "a watershed in my life."

How did he do it? What method drove his success?

You won't be surprised at the answers. The method to Eisenhower's success is outlined in the table of contents to this book.

Motivation. Discipline. Confidence. Sacrifice.

Ike prepared before he ever came to Fort Leavenworth; he understood the nature of the course long before his arrival. It was very much a series of problem-solving exercises, the type of challenges at which Eisenhower excelled. He understood intuitively what we now teach to every Army captain: Understanding and defining the challenge is half the battle.

Ike teamed with Leonard Gerow, a number one graduate of Fort Benning's Infantry School. Gerow would graduate eleventh at Leavenworth, later attain three-star rank, and, among other important postings, serve as commandant of the Leavenworth school.

Together the two men built a command post in the apartment, covering the walls with maps, installing a large worktable, and stacking bookshelves with class reference materials. Organization was key.

Execution was essential.

Unlike many of his competitive classmates, Ike paced himself. He played golf and was in bed by 9:30 on most nights. When he noticed others tightening under the pressure, he refocused on the task at hand. He found a clear head and common sense to be more effective than the attitude of academic drudgery consuming many of his classmates.

Remember "celebrate everything"?

Eisenhower and Gerow threw a graduation party at Kansas City's Muehlebach Hotel that lasted until dawn. By most accounts the celebration stretched the limits of the prohibition era, with Ike in the lead, just as he was first in his class.

As the news of Ike's upset achievement spread, telegrams and letters streamed in—including congratulations from his old pal, George S. Patton, who was already lining up leaders for the next war. Patton reminded Ike that the course was only a means to an end, noting that he was still working on the problems from his own days there—not to arrive at the school's solutions, but to determine how he would respond to challenges in the heat of battle.

World War II would come soon enough, and these two men would help win it.

War is the ultimate imperfection. The best one can hope for is to limit the damage, to keep the screwups to a sane level, and to survive to lick the wounds of victory. There can be glory, certainly, but it is always outweighed by the cost of its purchase.

The military is a great teacher. It is preparation for the underside of life, the fierce and the deadly. An effective military stretches its soldiers out of their comfort zone, always challenging, always changing, making order out of chaos. It is searching for truth in the most desperate situations and paying the price for miscalculation. It's a discipline that demands unwavering attention, intense focus, and often, violent action.

My goal with this work has been to translate the operative strategies of the United States Military, to make what we do and how we think accessible to anyone who will listen, and to present the strategies in a way that you can apply to life in general.

At its core, military training is an attitude—a can-do attitude—the power to overcome obstacles, think through problems, and perform at a consistently high level. It's an attitude that applies to everything.

The fifty Train Tough Strategies aren't just theory; they've worked for me and for the countless soldiers, sailors, airmen, and marines whom I've studied.

Take time to review these strategies. Key on the ones that resonate for you. Make them a part of your kit bag; install them into who you are so you can access them when the going gets tough—or when it's just plain time to get going.

Reveille sounded as I exited the Eisenhower apartment, America's reminder that life is a mission, each day a new quest.

Good luck with your mission. May the fifty Train Tough Strategies speed you on your quest.

1. **Commit to the Truth.** Subject all things to rigorous examination. The U.S. Military is a success story because, even despite the politics and rivalries, we have learned to seek and accept the truth about ourselves, our capabilities, and our enemies. The truth demands a response. That's when the real work begins.

2. **Prepare to Change.** What if just one area of your life improved as a result of the fifty strategies? Would it be worth it? What if you got fired up and got a new edge to life? If you're not prepared to change, to improve, you're wasting your time. Change involves accepting discomfort, so be prepared for some pain as you move to the next level.

3. **Accept Challenge.** Get used to meeting challenges, that's how muscle is built, both mental and physical. Military training is conducted under pressure. It's a life-or-death business. We're challenged mentally, physically, and spiritually. Meet the Train Tough Challenges as we move along. By the end, you'll be ready to take on the world.

4. **Harness the Power of Shock.** History is replete with cultures and human beings responding to shock. Think of the United States after Pearl Harbor. Shock got us focused. Shock got us moving. But the greater challenge is to conceptualize shocking scenarios and prepare accordingly. Get ahead of the shock curve and anticipate—

then feed off the energy. Attune to life's minishocks. Use them for motivation.

5. **Harness the Power of Belief.** Until you have harnessed your beliefs, you aren't ready to go on the quest. Without belief, life is a spectator sport. What do you believe? On what basis do you hold these beliefs? What you believe impacts your motivation. Your core beliefs are those truths you have validated over and over again. Know what they are.

6. **Inventory Your Assets.** What is the state of your mind? Your body? Your relationships? Your career? In the military we make inventory a continuous process. We always want to know where our people and equipment are, and whether they're ready for battle. Take stock of your assets, so you can fully access them on your quest.

7. **Develop a Quest Mentality.** You're not just sitting there, waiting for the world to come to you. You're on a quest. Know what that quest is. Ultimately, battles are won by going over to the offense, with all the risk of failure that comes with taking action. The quest mentality is one of the most powerful forces known to man. It will guide you through and around obstacles and into the unstoppable zone.

8. **Get Control of Your Environment.** As you develop discipline, you gain control of your mind and your environment. Uncluttering your mind gives you greater access to your mental source of power. Get out ahead of life and arrange things to support the goals you want to accomplish. The environment of continuous improvement is sustained by discipline.

9. **Establish Priorities.** Discipline is a routine followed with the total conviction of firmly established priorities. It requires a thinking process. Priorities help you know when you're not doing what you should be doing, like wasting time and energy on something that's counterproductive.

10. **Make Discipline a Habit.** Discipline has to become a habit. Consistency is the key. We know that every discipline affects every other discipline. The habits build on one another and become mutually reinforcing. The devil is in the details, so pay a lot of attention to

details. The good news it that solid habits eventually become second nature, a series of actions leading to enhanced performance. Ultimately, discipline allows and facilitates freedom.

11. **Understand the Components of Confidence.** Confidence is the result of preparation, experience, and tenacity. Preparation is a combination of hard work and the mental effort of planning. Tenacity is the mentality that thrives on adversity, made possible through a trained system of recovery. Confidence comes with experience—especially the experience of overcoming adversity. Desire fuels the process.

12. **Build Confidence Through Competence.** We're confident about what we do well. We learn best what we enjoy. *Confidence* and *competence* are 60 percent the same word—they're inextricably linked. Once you understand and accept that link, you're going to be tremendously more effective—and confident.

13. **Commit.** Your level of commitment is measured by sacrifice—the two go hand in hand. You can't walk off the field when you're committed; you accept a certain amount of pain, even fear. That's why, as human beings, one of our most treasured attributes is the ability to sacrifice. When we're committed, distractors lose their power. Our focus is on moving forward.

14. **Choose Sacrifice Over Shortcuts.** There's always a shortcut. Always. And let's face it, we all take the shortcut from time to time. The shortcut is the easier choice. But there are some situations where you must choose sacrifice in order to be effective. Sacrifice is uncomfortable; you have to see it as a cost of doing business. Because it's often counterintuitive, you have to consciously and rationally determine to make sacrifices.

15. **Choose "Anything" Over "Everything."** You can have anything you want, but not everything. Sacrifice is the operative concept here. Put a value on things, blowing ballast in order to achieve what's really important to you. Sacrifice is what makes "anything" possible.

16. **Have a Vision.** Get a picture in your mind of an ideal endstate. Vision is a specific destination, something that springs from your

principles and what you truly value. It's not what you *don't* want, it's what you *really* want. By definition, your quest implies a destination, and that destination is determined by vision.

17. **Master the Art of Strategic Design.** Will you use a direct or indirect approach? What is your center of gravity? What are the decisive points of your mission? Its culminating point? What is your exit strategy?

18. **Analyze Your Mission.** Mission analysis is the art of breaking down your mission into tasks, and analyzing your assets and limitations. Understand the difference between a fact and an assumption. Know the risks involved. Mission analysis is hard, organized, realistic thinking about an endeavor. It leads to planning, and ultimately achievement.

19. **Make Time Management a Priority.** Reverse-plan missions so you know how much time to allot to each task. Don't be a time hog—give others two-thirds of available planning time. Use "warning orders" to alert teammates to a new mission. Time is money; manage it as such.

20. **Learn How to Learn.** You learn what you want to learn. It's a question of desire; a sometimes uncomfortable process. It's not just sitting there—that's like getting stuck in a defensive mentality in the military. You've got to swing over to the offense and attack across a broad front—reading, listening, observing, performing. Attacking.

21. **Get into Self-Development.** Read. Study. Review. Improve. George S. Patton did. Open your own "Center for Lessons Learned" so you develop a mentality of constant learning. You won't know what you don't know until you ask the right questions. Developing your mind is the key to enhancing performance.

22. **Become a Problem Solver.** Problem solving is part art and part science, fueled by desire. Make sure your emotions are spurring you to action and not getting in the way. When you sense emotional dissonance, take a moment and think. See if you can rearrange things so you're accessing emotions as fuel and not putting out emotional wildfires. Ask yourself, "What would Swede Momsen do in a situation like this?"

23. **Define Problems.** The U.S. Military favors a methodical approach to problem solving, but we leave room for creativity. Brainstorm. Use visual centering to stay focused. Develop techniques for drawing out the thoughts and ideas of others. Watch out for groupthink. When working with a team, make sure you've got a solid definition of the problem you're trying to solve. It will help in your time management.

24. **Weave Ethical Considerations Into Everything.** It's a way of thinking and a way of life. It's a search for truth and an openness to examination. Establish what your values are. They may not be Army values, but the Army list is a great place to start. Loyalty. Duty. Respect. Selfless service. Honor. Integrity. Personal courage.

25. **Use the Ethical Decision-Making Process.** Examine ethical dilemmas for hidden opportunities. Get issues out in the open and deal with them. Watch out for rationalizations; they can be insidious and even become the norm. Define problems. Gather facts. Develop, analyze, and compare courses of action. Do what's right.

26. **Understand There Will Always Be Ethical Dilemmas.** Ethical dilemmas don't go away because you're the leader or because you've attained a certain level of enlightenment. In fact, they become more challenging. Leaders set the tone. Subordinates model leader behavior. Be proactive; challenge unethical traditions and reinforce what the team is doing right.

27. **Never Underestimate the Power of Organization.** We often take organization for granted. Living in chaos is sometimes our little way to fight the power. Organization seems boring and its processes laborious. But ultimately, organization is liberating. It eliminates confusion and saves precious time. It's an acquired taste.

28. **Begin Organization with Planning.** Think of a submarine, where the physical construction is predicated on mission, and equipment and personal effects are micro-organized. Everything is labeled and idiotproofed. The kid who couldn't put his toys away becomes a master organizer on a submarine. He learns to fit into the overall plan.

29. **Remember STTP.** Stuff, time and tasks, people. The more you have, the more you have to organize. Keep it simple. To find time, break it into small segments. Do the same with tasks. Then put the segments in order and prioritize. Keep a to-do list—and a "nudge list" for subordinates. Delegate whenever a subordinate can do a routine task with 75 percent proficiency.

30. **Understand the Psychology of High Performance.** Superior performance is attained by people who love what they're doing. It can also be generated by necessity. Embrace the work. Commit to never being outworked. Adopt a "no regrets" philosophy, the idea that you're going to do your best and let the chips fall where they may. It takes a lot of work to make it look easy.

31. **Always Be Prepared.** Pick your battles carefully. Then commit. Build a plan, one that creates the best synergy for the assets available. Visualize. Rehearse. Don't be surprised to be surprised.

32. **Finish Strong.** Take the ball and run with it. Maintain situational awareness. Focus. Adapt. Communicate. Run through the finish line, and be sure and set that line out far enough to encompass all the tasks that must be completed. The last 10 percent of any job is always the toughest, usually because nobody planned for it.

33. **Get Your Team on the Same Page.** Half of any job is communication. Everybody thinks they communicate, but they don't. Communication is work; it's not easy. You have to push and pull information—pull it out of sources and push it out to your people. When everybody knows the plan, the issues, current actions, and what the competition is up to, you'll be halfway home.

34. **Take Care of Your Line.** Every team has linemen, guys who do the hard work down in the trenches. In the military we call these men and women noncommissioned officers, or NCOs for short. Our system won't work without NCOs. They're indispensable role players, who oversee the day-to-day running of a ship or unit and rarely see the glory that seems to be reserved for officers. Every team has this kind of people. Make sure they're taken care of; don't wait until they're gone to appreciate them.

35. **Cross-Train Your Team.** Train as a team whenever possible. Team skills are different from individual skills. Get people out of their departments and into the big picture. This is how leaders are made and effective teams are built. Hire the best and train those who have the potential to be the best. Cross-train them to keep their comfort zone expanding, and your talent pool at maximum depth.

36. **Understand What People Don't Like About Their Leaders.** People hate it when they don't understand where they stand with the boss. They don't like feeling threatened, or having their time wasted. They don't like bosses who are pedantic or hypocritical. If you can avoid these pitfalls, you're on your way to becoming an effective leader.

37. **Understand What People Admire in Their Leaders.** People want to see courage, the courage to keep fighting when the whole thing seems to be coming down around your ears. Let people know where the goal line is. Make yourself a temporary equal once in a while and really, really listen. Be fair—that's harder than it seems at first blush. At the end of the day, people want your trust. If you can't give it right away, at least let people earn it.

38. **Dive into Leadership.** The first challenge of leadership is internal. There's no halfway—leadership is a full-time job. As a leader you shape culture, so always take the high road. You're in the inspiration business, so look for opportunities to show your people what you're made of. Learn to like people. Think. It's your mind that uniquely qualifies you for the position of leadership in which you find yourself. It's your obligation to think, strategize, and find the vision.

39. **Delegate, But Know What Not to Delegate.** You won't get far without the ability to delegate. The ability to solve problems is a nice skill to have, unless it gets in the way of leadership. Some things you can delegate; others you must hang onto. Don't delegate the people part of business. Stay involved in hiring, firing, evaluation, bonuses, and promotions. You can't lead without the led. Leaders are also the primary time managers for the operation. Good leaders show their involvement in people's time at every opportunity, and work to permeate their philosophy throughout the organization.

40. **Do the Easy Stuff.** Timeliness. Courtesy. Personal appearance. The nuances of career advancement can be quite complex, yet it's amazing how many people overlook the basics. Don't make a tough job tougher by missing the career discriminators that can make a difference. Be a problem solver. Be the best at something. Stay on top of the technological developments in your field. And for heaven's sake, do the easy stuff.

41. **Plan Your Career.** Seek responsibility. Take the tough jobs, the ones that will stretch you and show what you can do. Master the basics of managing your boss. Get up for special events—opportunities where you can shine. Dominate the meeting game, and never, ever underestimate inspections—even when they're called "assistance visits" or "surveys." Set the tone for these blessed events.

42. **Win the Battle for Bureaucratic Hill.** Bureaucracy is a significant part of the great game of life. Your effectiveness as a human being will be tested by how well you play this game. Bureaucrats thrive on wearing out opponents, so you'll have to be relentless. Take notes. Create the occasional crisis; bureaucrats hate to admit it, but crisis is what gets them going. Strike while the iron is hot, and don't be shy about going to the top when it's warranted—or suggesting that you might.

43. **"Move! Move! Move!"** Develop an active lifestyle. If it were easy, everybody would be doing it. But it's not. It takes aerobic exercise—like running, swimming, or cycling—to get that heart rate up. Keep trying new things; don't get bored. Keep track. Chart progress. Identify specific goals. Activity makes you better, and it builds confidence. It's a triumph over laziness and procrastination.

44. **Win the Battle of Diet and Weight Control.** Recognize your enemies, and build a plan to defeat them. Beer, doughnuts, and pizza come to mind. Build a supportive environment. Clear the refrigerator and cupboards of temptation. Shop carefully. Acquire new tastes. Cut portion sizes and second helpings. Eliminate alcohol at mealtime; it will break down your resistance every time. Drink plenty of water instead. Soldier through the first three days of your plan. Remember, *failure* is not a dirty word, *quitting* is a dirty word.

45. **Get More Sleep.** Most of the fifty strategies emphasize hard work and fighting your way out of a comfort zone. Now I'm telling you, emphatically, to get into your comfort zone and get more sleep. The vast majority of people need seven or eight hours a night—and we're not getting it. The right amount of sleep is essential for maintaining a positive attitude and emotional well-being. Build yourself a rest and relaxation plan. Develop a sleep routine, and make time to renew.

46. **Develop a Philosophy of Wealth.** Know where you fit on the security-versus-risk spectrum. Know yourself and what your challenges are in thinking about, defining, and acquiring wealth. Know what you want. Appreciate and protect what you have. If you say you value something, ask yourself, "What am I doing about it?" If you're not acting on your values, go back and reevaluate.

47. **Think of Money Management as a Board Game.** As in any board game, some occurrences are random, and you get penalized for not knowing the rules. You're rewarded for playing your hand wisely. It's imperative to understand the nuances of insurance, saving and spending fundamentals, investing, and taxes. What you don't know will cost you. Decide to become a student of the rules of wealth. Play hard.

48. **Give Something Back.** The evidence of what our forebears bequeathed to us is everywhere. Don't miss the joy of giving something back. Give. Give. Give. It's an attitude.

49. **Give Your Family Special Attention.** Regardless of how you define family, your family deserves special attention. Amazingly, many of the same techniques that work in the military also work in relationships—and life. Two of these are *organization* and *communication*. Half of the organizational challenge in the American family is simplification. Simplify, simplify, simplify. The challenge in communication is developing the ability to listen. Actions speak louder than words, except for words of praise.

50. **Work for Balance in Your Relationships.** Relationships require constant grooming to survive the pressures of the present culture. Work for balance. There may be times when career demands are

going to take precedence over your relationships. Prepare for those times. Organization, teamwork, problem solving, discipline—all the things we've emphasized—will help you through. But, as in everything else, nothing relieves you of the responsibility to think.

Just because you haven't served in the military doesn't mean you can't master the same mentality and life skills that come with military training. People do it all the time. It's very easy for me to get on the same wavelength with people of power who've never had military training, but who exude the same characteristics of motivation, discipline, confidence, and sacrifice.

Al Davis, whom I wrote about in *Train Tough the Army Way,* is a classic example. Al's a former teammate of mine who coached college basketball and is now a successful financial consultant. Al exudes tremendous enthusiasm coupled with a unique ability to communicate. He tells it like it is. He could have been a great drill sergeant, general officer, or special forces operative. In fact, whenever he calls and one of my kids answers, he'll adopt a military alias and have them snap to. They always think it's the Pentagon calling Dad for some deadly mission.

I was recently extolling the virtues of my fitness program when Al cut me off.

"It's not good enough," he said, emphasizing each word.

I was take aback.

"But Al," I explained, "I'm swimming a mile every other day, running, cycling, lifting weights. . . ."

"It's not . . . good . . . enough."

Nobody talks to the colonel that way. Except Al.

He went on to pick apart my exercise program and rebuild it in a way that made more sense. Sometimes I think I spent my entire military career preparing for his training programs.

Al has more military panache than I will ever have.

You don't necessarily have to do a thing in order to understand and learn from it.

Hopefully, this book has been a step in that direction.

Remember, in America's Military we study everything. We're studying you. We want to know what works in America, and how we can leverage your endless creativity. Our enemies do the same thing; we just do it faster.

You're tougher than you think.

The challenges you overcome today are preparation for the challenges of tomorrow. You're stronger than you think.

I'm reminded of a sign I saw on the premises of Navy Seal training:

THE ONLY EASY DAY WAS YESTERDAY.

I wish you peace, love, and the challenge of victory.

ACKNOWLEDGMENTS

Special thanks to Therese Carmack, Van Crouch, Al Davis, Bill Hart, and Galen McPherson for sharing their stories through interviews and for their words of inspiration.

I pay tribute to the late Nick Winter, general counsel at American Biography and my friend, comrade-in-arms, and counselor. His advice was critical in the early going, and he was always there in a crisis. A writer himself, he understood the narrow path we follow and was always ready with a word of encouragement for a fellow traveler. I learned a lot from Nick.

Tom Bender, who serves as the West Coast coordinator for the Train Tough Strategies, did a terrific job reviewing each chapter, providing the kind of tough-love feedback that only a brother can.

It was a pleasure to work with Jacqueline Flynn, senior editor at Amacom Books, and managing editor Andy Ambraziejus. Their enthusiasm and guidance sustained me throughout. Thanks also to Christine Furry at North Market Street Graphics for her fine work.

I would like to thank my dad, Sam Bender, and the following friends and associates whose help was invaluable: Mary Beth Arms, Dena Bachman, Steve Brown, Marlin and Linda Cone, Marv Decker, Gary Eckert, Nelson Elliott, Alvin Hoy, Kimberly Howard, Rosa Isern, Art and Linda Jones, Pat King, Kate Klemish, Norma Lamp, Betsy Lancefield Lane, Warren and Anneliese Lott, Bob Malkemes, Tim McCarthy, Donna Martin, Frank Moyer, Joe Occhuizzo, Laurie Van Ouden, Pete and Lyn Pierce, Dawn Rachelle, Shirley Rickett, Clarence and Ebby Roberts, Norman Robbins, Rosalyn Spring, and Karla Thrush.

Recounting of the sacrifice at Valley Forge was assisted by C. Brian Kelly's *Best Little Stories from the Revolution* and Robert Leckie's *George Washington's War: The Saga of the American Revolution*. The Web site at www.npca.org was also helpful.

Our Jungle Road to Tokyo, by Robert Eichelberger, is an excellent first-person account of the Battle of Buna, with the Web site at www. worldwariihistory.info filling in important details.

Background on the life of Harry Truman was gleaned from David McCullough's *Truman* and the American Experience film *Truman*, with transcript available at www.pbs.org.

Roger H. Nye's *The Patton Mind* is a superb illustrated guide to how Patton thought and how he studied. It shows a new side of the great warrior.

Peter Maas does us all a great service by bringing Swede Momsen to our attention in *The Terrible Hours: The Man Behind the Greatest Submarine Rescue in History*. It is inspirational reading at its finest. The Web sites at www.onr.navy.mil and www.fleetsubmarine.com were also informative.

The generosity and dedication of small-town America rings true in Bob Greene's *Once Upon a Town: The Miracle of the North Platte Canteen*. It's a great read on a uniquely American phenomenon.

I used three sources in discussing Tiger Woods: *The Chosen One: Tiger Woods and the Dilemma of Greatness*, by David Owen; *Training a Tiger: A Father's Guide to Raising a Winner in Both Golf and Life*, by Earl Woods with Pete McDaniel; and *Playing Through: Straight Talk on Hard Work, Big Dreams and Adventures with Tiger*, by Earl Woods with Fred Mitchell.

The Right Words at the Right Time, by Marlo Thomas and friends, is a great collection of positive reminiscences, in which I found the words on confidence by Mary Matalin, quoting her father.

Fred Barnes's article, "How Tommy Franks Won the War," published in *The Weekly Standard*, is a cogent explanation of Gulf War II, and Charles Moskos's article, "Overcoming Race: Lessons for American Society" in the February 2003 issue of *Military Officer* is a superb explanation of how the Army leverages team play.

The Yamashita case study is based on William Branch's 1990 study project, "The Yamashita Decision," published by the U.S. Army War College.

The following organizations also deserve thanks: Mid-Continent Public Library, Kansas City Public Library, Military Officer Association, U.S. Army Combined Arms Center and Fort Leavenworth, Park Hill High School, U.S. Army Combined Arms Research Library, The Writer's Place, U.S. Army War College, Maple Woods Community College, University of Missouri at Kansas City, Weatherby Lake Writers' Guild, Navy District Recruiting Command—Kansas City, Fleet Center San Diego, and the hospitable crews of the USS *John C. Stennis* and USS *Portsmouth*.

This work would not have been possible without my family: Jim with chapter editing, Bob with www.TrainTough.com, Lisa with the vignette on communication, and Matt casting aspersions on us all. Thanks to my wife Heidi for all her help, not the least of which was her work on Chapter 16, "Relationships." It may be the toughest game in town, but it's also the most rewarding.

INDEX

the master architect of the famed triangle offense. *Trial* provides an in-depth analysis of the Michael Jordan phenomenon, the bittersweet presence of Dennis Rodman, the migration of a coaching staff to Tinseltown—and a world championship. Los Angeles Laker coach Phil Jackson wrote the foreword to *Trial,* and Bender was one of the few persons allowed into his Laker basketball practices.

A physical fitness and sports fanatic, Bender achieved the Army's maximum physical fitness score thirty-five consecutive times—and recently completed his seventy-fifth season in team sports. His range of experiences provides a solid backdrop for his commentaries on business, health and fitness, relationships, and life. He communicates with a unique style, and the confidence of someone who's been there.

For more information on Mark Bender and the Train Tough Strategies, visit www.TrainTough.com.

ABOUT THE AUTHOR

Mark Bender is vice president and executive editor of American Biography and the creator and chief spokesperson for the Train Tough Strategies.

A 1996 graduate of the U.S. Army War College, Bender holds a graduate degree in military art and science and is the author of *Watershed at Leavenworth*, the dynamic story of Dwight Eisenhower's rise to power after graduating first in his class at the Army's Command and General Staff College. *Watershed* details the strategy and tactics Eisenhower employed in mastering the highly competitive yearlong course, a course his superiors told him he would "probably fail." Bender borrows heavily from his own military experience in analyzing the Eisenhower strategy and has appeared as a subject matter expert on A&E's *Biography*.

Bender completed a 24-year active duty career in the U.S. Army in 1998. He served with both military intelligence and mechanized infantry units, but his primary focus was on soldier resources, where he gained valuable experience in leadership and management, team building, and customer service. He was selected "Officer of the Year" for Headquarters, Allied Forces Central Europe in 1980. From 1990 to 1992 Bender served in Nuremberg, Germany, assisting in the preparation of over 10,000 soldiers for Operation Desert Storm. He was selected "Instructor of the Year" for the Army's premier junior executive course in 1994.

A much-in-demand motivational speaker, Bender has addressed numerous sports teams, including the New York Yankees baseball team. He has been interviewed on radio from coast to coast, and his comedy has entertained live audiences in the United States and Europe. His 2002 book, *Train Tough the Army Way: 50 Sports Strategies to Out-Think, Out-Train, and Out-Perform Your Competition*, details how military strategy and tactics can impact the world of sport. Yankee great Bobby Murcer, with whom Bender has shared many experiences, wrote the foreword.

His 2000 book, *Trial By Basketball—The Life and Times of Tex Winter*, took him inside the Chicago Bulls dynasty years as he explored the life of